THE BRIDGE ... TO THE OTHER SIDE

by Vikee Vaughn

©1988 by Vikee Vaughn

All rights reserved. No part of this book may be reproduced without the express written permission of the copyright holder. Permission is hereby granted to legitimate literary reviewers to reproduce excerpts in their reviews.

International Standard Book Number: 0-944534-01-5
Library of Congress Catalogue Card Number: 89-45150
Printed in the United States of America

Published in 1988 by Authors Unlimited

Reprinted in 1991 by Diamond Publishing

P.O. Box 8580
Stockton, California
95208

TO JASON

Who truly showed me that love is never separated...

With acknowledgement and deep appreciation

For all the loving help and information from Richard's and my guides, family, all those who contributed, and our friends from "above"...

FOREWORD

"Human life never stands still, nor comes to an end. On leaving the physical body the departed spirit enters into the soul and spiritual worlds to continue living, and to enjoy their kingdoms."

From "Life After Death" by Hanna Jacob Doumette, 1938

Ever since I can remember, I wanted to know "why" about things I did not understand. As an only child, and alone most of the time, I pondered and read a great deal. I only believed in the good, and my pink cloud world seemed to protect me.

Many years later when my father died of cancer, my sense of failure to help him brought me to the sharp realty of life and death.

By this time I was married, with a teenage boy and girl, I thought I knew many answers, but why, I asked myself, did such a good and wonderful man we loved so much have to die? Just like the unexplained answers of sudden deaths and tragedies to those all over the world. If God was such a great and loving God, then why? It would not seem logical that the greatness of God, who is life and all-intelligence, would take away a part of that life, especially leaving so many with such little time on earth. I knew within my being there had to be more...

I searched, and researched. I analyzed the logic that if we did live before, and then continued in the cycle of unending life, it would be natural to go on living after our so called "death".

In our life here, important events, emotions and sudden deaths could be explained easier if they were "carry-overs" from the far past. This would be the result of the karmic law of cause and effect. Backing this up is St. Paul from Galatians 6:7 "Whatsoever a man soweth that shall he also reap". It could be then better understood that man had more control over his life than thought before. He did not have to feel a "victim" of God's so called wrath, especially if He was an all-loving, all-encompassing God. It would be impossible to balance out all man's deeds in one lifetime.

Man has to begin to take more account of his part in responsibility of his thoughts and actions. He needs to consider that his own attitudes and beliefs can have a part in drawing certain circumstances. Just as he is the effect from his childhood fears and surroundings, he should be open to the thought that emotions and the drawing felt to certain people can go back even further than birth. There have been countless books written to verify this if one would care to pursue.

This book is the story of how a family death increased the desire to learn more truths of the beyond, and the steps of growth that unfolded.

I had to have my own proof. I prayed that if there was a way for my father to reveal he was still existing, something would happen. My children, wise beyond their years, and I were close to God. We asked for help. The thought came as if in answer. We decided to try and reach out in faith... to tap the unknown...

Table of Contents

PART I THE STORY

ONE	How It All Started	3
TWO	The Guides' Messages Begin	15
THREE	Parting of the Ways	23
FOUR	New Beginning	27
FIVE	The Growing Years	33
SIX	Life In The Valley	40
SEVEN	Las Vegas	45
EIGHT	The Return	49
NINE	Goodbye, Jason	53
TEN	The Messages Begin Again	59
ELEVEN	The Story of Martha	75
TWELVE	Richard and Lynne	87
THIRTEEN	Keeping in Touch With Jason	91
FOURTEEN	Richard Returns	97

PART II THE CONTACTS

FIFTEEN	The Messages Continue	103
SIXTEEN	Communication From Famous People	113
SEVENTEEN	Other Famous People from the Past	123
EIGHTEEN	From the Unknown	133
NINETEEN	From the Higher Ones	139
TWENTY	Beings From Outer Space	153
TWENTY-ONE	Questions to the Other Side	173
EPILOGUE		193

PART I
"THE STORY"

CHAPTER ONE

How It All Started

There were four of us holding hands around the table. It was dark except for the candles burning. Our eyes were closed, we were waiting... waiting for something to happen. I blinked a quick glance around the room. Candle shadows were flickering. My daughter Annette was sitting across from me, her eyes closed tightly. This moment was very important to her. It was going to be the night of answers, the night of truth for her — whether her grandfather was really living in the beyond. Before he died of cancer several months back she had nearly worshipped him. She had to know what happened to him.

Sitting between Annette and myself on my left, was Annette's friend of many years, Jenny. Her face was tense. She needed her own special proof. Jenny's brother had died from an accident the year before.

On my right was my son, Richard, sixteen years in age but not in mind. He had many depths that were yet to surface. As we sat in silence waiting, eyes closed, my thoughts drifted back to several months ago:

* * *

Richard, hesitant but excited, had come into my bedroom where I was reading.

"Yes, what is it?" I asked.

"Mother," he began, "I have something important to tell you, but I don't know how to begin. It's about grandfather."

I put my book down, knowing Richard had been grieving since my father's recent death. Having prayed so hard for him to live, Richard felt personal failure when his grandfather died.

"What about grandfather?"

"Well, he just now came to me in my room. You probably think I was dreaming, but I wasn't! I really wasn't!" he exclaimed.

"What do you mean?" I said with a start.

"He just appeared in my room and was standing near me. It was kind of hazy. He looked terrific, Mother. He was smiling. He looked happy. He said he came to thank me for my prayers because they helped him find the peace he was looking for. He is much happier where he is now and feels no more pain. He is going to help me and watch over me and all of us!" Richard's eyes shone with excitement.

I was speechless, not sure of what to say.

Do you believe me Mother?'" His presence was so peaceful. It was real. Please believe me!"

Before I spoke, I thought back on Richard's growing years. A very normal child, he liked all sports, participated in Cub Scouts, always had pets around, was class president in the sixth grade, and played saxophone in the school band. He nearly always made the honor roll. Even if he was on the messy side about his room, he was dependable about rules. He was never rowdy or broke a toy. Richard seemed to take more pleasure in pleasing than being rebellious. He was protective of his pretty sister, Annette, nearly two years younger.

No, he was not one to make up stories for attention. He was much too busy learning things on his own.

"If you say this is true, I believe you," I answered.

So that is how it began, I was either going to reject what Richard had said, or be open-minded. I chose the latter.

I mentioned this incident to a good friend (one I knew before Richard was born). Yvette was a very intuitive person. When Richard was a baby she had called him "grandpa", because he seemed like such a little wise old soul she had said.

Yvette not only believed Richard but admitted a similar experience I had not been aware of. Her own mother, after passing on, had appeared, and assured her she was okay. We now had a deeper mutual topic to share.

The thought came to me to go to the library for books pertaining to life after death. The various subjects all fascinated me — books on ESP, dreams, astral projection, psychic experiences and reincarnation.

The first I read were by Edgar Cayce, referred to as the sleeping prophet. In his sleep state, helpful information poured out regarding natural healing methods that had remarkable results. As he became more well-known, thousands of people were helped. In his sleep state readings, he explained the cause of deep-rooting problems in this earth life, which usually came from a past life.

I was introduced to the term "karma," an ancient far-eastern name for the law of cause and effect. It is interesting that the same reference was made in the Bible: "What ye sow, so also shall ye reap". In other words, we are repaid for either the good or the bad we have been accumulating from past lifetimes, and are reborn on earth to progress and overcome our bad decisions or "sins". It became clear why some people have so many problems, or find themselves in such unhappy situations; why some are taken from this earth so young, and others live such a long life. We are constantly drawing to ourselves either good or bad, due to our thinking behavior. *faith* or *fear* govern our lives.

This new realization changed my life.

While absorbing these new thoughts, I received a phone call from a dear friend from high school days. We had been in each other's wedding. She was going through a divorce and after all these years had tracked me down. Her daughter was near my Annette's age.

I drove down the peninsula from San Francisco to visit her that next week, anxious to catch up on our lives. As our conversation was brought up to the present, I brought up the incident of Richard's vision of my father. Her acceptance was amazing. She was eager to relate to someone that was open, that she had been getting messages from a guide in the spirit world through the Ouija board. He said he had been a past love from another lifetime and was coming through to help her. She received answers from the board about questions she could not possibly have known. After more conversation we worked the board together.

The Ouija board pointer, or planchette, began spelling out words. Some force not coming from our hands was actually moving it around. Different questions were answered by Lorna's guide, Alexander. Then another spirit came through named Robin. He said he was the father of a school friend of Richard's. He had died six years ago. He wished to be a helper, and hoped I could be of help to his son when possible. (Months later, Richard did try to approach his friend about his father's spirit being around to help, but he refused to be open about it.)

I wanted to stay longer but felt I should go home because my children would wonder where I was. Robin's message then said the children would be delayed in coming home and not to worry. It turned out as Robin had said. I was fascinated.

Within a few days another friend, Della, stopped by, bringing a book she was very excited about, *A Search for Truth*, by Ruth Montgomery. The subtitle said: "A startling report on personal experience in the psychic world". Ruth Montgomery, a journalist, was used to dealing in facts. Some time after her father passed away, he came to her, first through the famous medium, Arthur Ford, then later through her own typewriter. Ford became her guide, which led to new information and enlightenment previously foreign to her. For me it was another confirmation of life after death.

Della started coming to my house regularly to spend time working the Ouija board for answers. I asked my guide, Robin, about my father. He said my father was going to school and learning more about soul development and being a helper. He would come to us later.

The days that followed became more exciting as I started getting more messages from the other side. I knew the Ouija board had been used in many ways down through the years, from simple family entertainment to receiving messages from spirits. I read where some entities moving the planchette were earthbound, not releasing emotions carried over from death. Some were mischievous, some were sincere. Some wished to control. We found that by raising our vibration in prayer, we could be protected from any questionable influences.

By lifting our consciousness to a higher level, we opened the way for sincere helpers and relatives to reach us. Prayer sends a path of light, and we began to receive messages of guidance. Insight into past lives also was revealed.

It was obvious that the energy force moving the planchette was not from our hands. By many avenues man progresses into higher knowledge when he is ready. Going to church does not mean a person is growing spiritually or becoming enlightened. The heart must be open to the truths of wisdom from many sources.

During one of our sessions, I asked about my father again. The answer was, "Be patient. He will come soon. He is still going through preparation." He had progressed because we knew of his continued existence. This had given him incentive to learn and communicate. While on earth my father was not a believer in the hereafter. More than once we had disagreed on that subject, so my reaching him was especially meaningful to me. After he died, when the children passed their grandfather's recliner chair, many times they felt his presence strongly. "Grandpa is around," they would say. Sometimes Annette would go to the record player and put on his favorite record, by Ted Lewis, singing "When My Baby Smiles At Me", or "Me And My Shadow". She would dance around happily in front of the recliner. There were many moments of "closeness".

* * *

It is amazing how much the mind can flash back in just moments, I reflected as I thought about the events that had brought us together this night. And this would be the final proof.

Then, ever so slightly, the table moved, making the candles flicker. Suddenly I felt my son's hand on mine becoming stronger as he gripped it.

My heart jumped! That squeeze triggered a memory of the last day I saw my father when I knew he was dying. I would never forget that moment. It was my birthday. He had put a twenty dollar bill in my hand and squeezed it hard, as though he didn't ever want to let go.

I leaned forward, staring at Richard. His face had become more drawn and older looking! Then I heard a rasping sound come out of his mouth.

"D-o-n-n-a..." came forth. "D-o-n-n-a..."

My father had always called me that. An officer overseas in the war, he had come back to find my mother had been calling me Vikee, then had it changed.

"You will always be Donna to me," he had said.

As the candles flickered, I called out: "Daddy, oh daddy, it really is you!"

Everyone around the table became excited. They had seen the change in my son's facial expression. Feeling heavy with emotion, I asked, "Daddy, are you alright?"

"Yes... D-o-n-n-a... I am r-e-a-l-l-y h-e-r-e-. Am f-i-n-e..."

It seemed very difficult for him to speak. Words in a deep whisper came slowly and broken. He sounded far, far away.

"Can-'t t-a-l-k... l-o-n-g..." he rasped, "am... b-e-i-n-g... h-e-l-p-e-d... t-o-... be... h-e-r-e..."

There were so many things I wanted to ask him that my mind almost went blank with excitement. I managed to get out: "What do you see for us ahead daddy?"

"Don't... w-o-r-r-y... w-i-l-l... be a-r-o-u-n-d... You... a-r-e... b-e-i-n-g... w-a-t-c-h-e-d... o-v-e-r... all... of... you..."

"We love you so much," I said. "We are so happy you came to us! How wonderful to know you are still living and can be so close to us. We often felt you were."

"Yes... do... n-o-t... be... a-f-r-a-i-d... you are al-ways... pro-tect-ed... ke-ep your... faith... ne-v-er s-t-o-p be-l-i-e-v-i-n-g...... h-a-v-i-n-g... p-ro-b-l-e-m-s... have to g-o-... l-o-v-e... y-o-u-......"

"Wait!" I yelled. There were so many questions I still wanted to ask. I wanted to cry.

Suddenly I felt a difference in Richard's hand clasp. It had changed back to normal. Then I saw his facial expression change. My dear father was gone...

Though I spoke his name, Richard seemed unconscious. Finally, he opened his eyes. We gathered around him. He looked dazed.

"Richard, what happened?" I exclaimed.

After slowly regaining his composure, he described what had taken place: "It's hard to believe. It was so strange. While I was holding hands with both of you, glancing at Annette and myself I saw grandfather coming down to me. I came up out of my body and we hugged. Then he came into my body while I went upwards, toward a beautiful and bright light in the form of a cross. I saw Grandma Lewis (my mother's mother who died when Richard was a toddler)."

"How on earth did you know it was her?" I asked. "You couldn't possibly remember her."

"I don't know how, but I knew it was my Grandma Lewis. Then we hugged." As Richard described her, I knew it was my laughing, wonderful grandmother alright!

He went on to say: "There were lots of people around who said they had much to tell me. I could still see grandfather down below in my body as I looked down. Then I remember floating off with some heavenly people. I had never felt like that before. It was so exhilarating. Then it seemed hazy... I can't remember after that, except I did not want to come back. They told me I must, that there was special work ahead of me."

Jenny had been listening intently. She asked, "Were you scared? And did you see my brother?"

"Oh no, I wasn't scared, it was wonderful. And I did see Roger. He looked very happy. He was with other kids around his age. He was riding a bicycle and waving!"

There were tears in Jenny's eyes, remembering her twelve-year-old brother, and her sadness when he died. "I wish I could have seen him" she said quietly.

"He is around when you think of him, Jenny. Roger doesn't want you to be sad because he is in a happy place. He has friends and relatives there with him and he is busy growing and learning. They have so many activities there; and yet he makes his presence felt to you and your family whenever he can."

"Really?" asked Jenny, amazed.

"Roger meets you in dreams, even if you don't remember. I found out so much," he added.

"Let's try this again soon," said Jenny. "Maybe Roger will come through like your grandfather!"

"This was a special happening. They told me not to do this again for now. Not just anyone can come through like grandfather did. He had a lot of help there, because it was important for us to have the proof he was still living, not only him, but others. This was a beautiful gift to us tonight so we could understand many new things." He looked at all of us.

"I do remember them telling me there must be more spiritual preparation on my part to effectively connect with the higher vibrations. Lower spirits could cause problems and interfere. They have told me not to pursue this now, but to go on with my schooling and life activities. But we are to pray more, and we will be guided and protected."

* * *

In the days that followed, Annette kept saying that she wanted to see her grandfather, to feel more of his closeness. After all, her brother had gone beyond that. Though I told her we were to let it go for now, she kept after me. So one day when my friend Della and I were working the Ouija board I asked about it.

For the first time, my father came through on the board! He verified all the things Richard had said about his recent experience. He said it was too difficult to come forth the way he had, through Richard, that we could communicate easier through the board or writing on paper.

It seemed to be so important to Annette, that my father prescribed the following method for her to contact him: Annette was to lie down and I was to talk softly to her in a meditative state until she drifted off. After she was completely still I took hold of her arm; it was limp. She was smiling, though far away.

Just then a knock came at the front door! I jumped up and shut the bedroom door to greet the friends who had arrived. We talked in the livingroom. Before they left, the bedroom door opened and Annette appeared, relaxed and smiling. When they left I couldn't wait to ask her if she was alright and did she remember anything.

"Oh mother, I saw grandfather! He came to me! We hugged, and then he took me by the hand. It was like, I was pulled upward. I looked down and I could see earth with darkness all around it. Then it was as if we were coming up through the darkness into lighter clouds. It became lighter and lighter. Then I heard beautiful music! It was coming from a merry-go-round like I've never seen. Rainbow colors were all around it. I saw birds all colors and little animals having fun playing. And flowers so pretty and I could even smell them. Then I saw some kids around my age playing games and doing different activities. Some were painting, some were even building things. It was wonderful to watch. But the time seemed to go by too fast and before I knew it Grandfather said it was time to go back. I didn't want to, but he promised he would be around when I needed him. He said I should concentrate on getting good grades at school and being loving and kind to everyone. Mother, I'm so happy for that visit, I will never forget it!"

Who is to say whether Annette's trip was only a dream, or whether it was real...?

CHAPTER TWO

The Guides' Messages Begin

My exuberant friend, Della came over often and we started writing down the messages that came through on the Ouija board. Most were helpful guidance.

One day we received a message to pray for California. At first we laughed over this, but, strangely enough, the very next day we heard that an earthquake had been predicted in the Bay Area where we lived. We thought: What good would our prayers do?

As time went on, we realized that prayer is a very powerful force. Every prayer sent out into the atmosphere with faith and conviction eliminates more negative vibrations. Even though we didn't know if it would help that much, we did a lot of praying to replace negative or earthquake vibrations with positive energy and harmony.

The earthquake never happened. We weren't naive enough to think we were the ones that stopped it, but it was the beginning of learning how important it is to replace negative thoughts and reports from the news medium with positive affirmations.

Another time I was planning on flying to Los Angeles to visit my mother who had remarried and moved there after my father's death. The day of my flight, Della came over. As she walked in she said, "Vikee, I am sure sorry, but you are not going to Los Angeles today."

"Oh yes I am!" I declared. "My mother is not well, and it would really disappoint her if I didn't come. Now, what's this all about?"

"I don't know," Della went on, "but I got a message that said you were not to go. Let's try the board."

I was reluctant because I didn't want to have any opposition or have anyone tell me what to do. Then I flashed back to a recent incident:

It was when I felt I should start looking for a job to help out. My husband's moving business was slow. The board had spelled out "No, do not look for work now. Spend more time in prayer and study of metaphysics."

It seemed every effort was blocked that was put forth to go to work. Then one morning a friend called, knowing I had been looking for any kind of work. She had just quit her job at a nice dinner house by the Oakland Airport overlooking the bay. I thought that this must be an opportunity or she wouldn't have called. I called the Blue Dolphin restaurant and talked to the manager. They hadn't a fill-in yet and told me to come in, and wear a black skirt and white blouse.

When I called Della about it she laughed and said, "I'll bet something happens and you don't start work." That evening as I put my apron on at the restaurant and started to go out on the floor to work, a man tapped me on the shoulder and asked me if I belonged to the union. I said, "Well, I haven't had a chance to join yet." He was a union official. Apparently that wasn't good enough. I had to leave the floor. The girls there said that had never happened before. I went home and called Della. She giggled and said, "Well, Vikee did you get the message?"

* * *

My thoughts came back to the kitchen where Della and I were about to work the board. My guide, Robin, said it was very important I stay home this weekend. Also, to keep my daughter at home for her protection as she was in danger of an accident. On top of that they added, my mother would need me more next weekend. I became very upset as I had looked forward to seeing her,

Just then the front door flew open and Annette came running in from school, sobbing.

"Oh mother, I almost got killed! On the way home from school I stepped off the curb and from out of nowhere a car came right at me! It was like something then yanked me back on the curb, or I would have been hit!"

Della and I looked at each other. I knew I wasn't going to Los Angeles that weekend.

The interesting part about this incident was that when I flew to Los Angeles the following weekend, I saved my mother's life.

The doctors had given up on my mother eighteen years ago. Due to an aneurysm in her head, Mayo clinic had given her less than a year to live. Since the doctors couldn't help her anymore, she turned to God as her doctor and put Him in charge. Her new attitude had given her a more positive outlook on life with faith and determination. She became stronger and was able to function normally. She continued to drive her Cadillac around, play bridge masterfully and always kept that outgoing exuberance of life. This made her beauty radiate even more, her blue eyes sparkled, her dark hair shone. She even visited the hospitals and played chess with patients not given long to live, talking them into getting well. She was a remarkable woman.

The weekend I flew to see her I could tell she was not her jovial self, yet was happy to see me. After her husband, Sandy, left for work the next morning I decided to fix breakfast and brought it to her in bed. I was thinking about all the fun things we did over the years as I set her tray down. I looked over at her face and realized she wasn't breathing! I shook her but there was no change! When I raced to the phone to call an ambulance I was stopped short. I could hear my grandmother Lewis's voice. She said, "Don't phone. Go to your mother now! Call her back. PRAY. Call her back... NOW!"

I ran to the bed. "Mother!" I yelled, throwing my arms around her. I kept calling her name and telling her we needed and loved her as the tears rolled down my cheeks. After what seemed liked an eternity but was only a few minutes, she opened her eyes and smiled slowly at me.

"Vikee... I think I died. I felt a strong pulling into a dark tunnel. There was a cord attached to me. (the cord she was referring to is actually called the "silver cord", the umbilical attachment, and death occurs when it is severed).

My mother continued, "As I started to go through a misty haze and let go of that cord I heard your voice calling me. It made me stop. Your voice was the only thing that made me hang on. Oh Vikee, what an experience. I'm weak, but I feel better now. But you know, I wasn't afraid to let go. I was not afraid of dying. I felt peace waiting for me."

* * *

Sometime after I had returned home, my daughter and a neighbor girl named Gayle decided to work the Ouija board. A spirit named William Henderson slowly spelled out his name. He was in distress and looking for his daughter. The girls asked me if I would help. When we took out the board he was right there asking for our help. Gayle had felt that "someone" was around several times before. William scrawled out that he had killed his wife in a jealous rage and then killed himself. After awakening from a deep sleep he was returning to seek his daughter. Gayle's family had only lived in the house a few years and knew nothing about the history of the house.

The girls and I held hands and prayed for William. I tried to help him release himself from both the tragedy and the house.

"You will be guided to your daughter when you become open to Divine help," I told him. I begged him to turn to his loving guides who would show him more about truth and forgiveness in understanding his past life experience. "If you choose to remain where you are in your concepts you will remain miserable and lost," I said. Spirits that keep their memories locked into their trauma when departing are what we know as ghosts. Prayer can help these trapped souls. More people need to know the power of prayer.

Our prayers must have helped. The next day I received a phone call from Jenny's mother, Jane. She worked the board from time to time, sometimes getting a message from her son Roger.

Jane asked me if I knew a William Henderson who came through. I told her about the incident with him.

"I knew it must have been something like that, the way he described who you were (the lady of light, with the prayers)." She added, "He wanted you to know how much he appreciates your help and prayers and that he is going on."

How fascinating that someone totally unaware of this happening received a message for me! I was amazed.

The next evening my guide Robin, came through the board; "I have appreciated your prayers for my son, and hope you continue, but because you have helped another soul elevate his consciousness you have been given a higher guide. His name is King William. He asks that you use the pen now instead of this method, and continue to be open. I will come to you from time to time. Your friend, Robin."

* * *

A few months later another unusual occurrence happened. My husband and I had driven with our children to meet my mother and step father for a vacation together. We had stayed overnight in San Diego the last night of our trip. I remember feeling as I looked out to the ocean from our hotel verandah that it seemed like my husband and I were like two strangers. A sadness came over me.

The next day after arriving back to Los Angeles, my mother had an attack, a form of stroke, and was rushed to the hospital. The neurosurgeon, Dr. Kent, wanted to do an angiogram. A few years back she had such bad effects from one that she made us promise we would never let any doctor perform another. She felt she would not survive it.

During her semiconscious state, we tried to explain to Dr. Kent why we wouldn't agree to another angiogram. He was not understanding and extremely rude, even yelling at us before he stomped off.

After my mother was taken out of intensive care and began recovering, we drove back to Hayward but kept her in our constant prayers.

A few days after we returned I took Annette to the dentist. While sitting in the outer room waiting, all of a sudden I had a strong desire to reach in my purse and pull out my pen. I grabbed some paper and scribbling out on it was "Go to your mother! Now! Pray!" Alone in the waiting room I closed my eyes and sent all the light and healing forces I could to her. I couldn't wait to get home. When I called the hospital, she finally answered her extension, "Vikee! You saved my life today! Thank God you came!"

"Mother, what do you mean?"

"That mean Dr. Kent came in my room and started giving me a bad time. He demanded I have an angiogram. When I insisted that I would get well without one, he became so angry he yelled that I would die without one. Then he walked out. Something happened inside me and I felt I was starting to slip away, he upset me so much. Then, thank heavens, Vikee you came right into my room and started telling me not to listen to the doctor, I was going to do just fine without the angiogram. You convinced me that I should not let him upset me and to have faith in my healing."

I could hardly believe what I heard.

"Mother," I said slowly, "I couldn't have been in your room. I'm still in Hayward."

"Dear," she insisted, "It was too real. I know you were here. You had on a peach colored cotton dress, it was sleeveless. You had dangly earrings on to match."

I listened astounded. That was exactly what I was wearing and... she had never seen it on me.

My mother did get well. She lived ten years after that. Just a case in point: Dr. Kent, temper and all, died of a heart attack the following year.

I did not understand what had taken place when my mother was so certain she really saw me in her room that day. Later, I found out that what happened has happened many times before, to many people. It seems that in very stressful and emotional situations, the subconscious plea for help can send energy forces that can make one's specific need a reality.

CHAPTER THREE

Parting of the Ways

I had been married eighteen years when I started receiving messages from my guides. I couldn't imagine what had happened to the many years that had flown by. Now I had loving, nearly grown children, ready to make their own way in life soon.

My husband Dean worked hard trying to make ends meet. He was able to earn enough so that I could stay home most of the time. That is the way he wanted it. I worked part time when needed but was there when Annette and Richard came home after school. I remembered back to my childhood, with my mother working nights and not being there; it was especially important for me to be there now.

After Annette got older she told me how much it meant to her that I was home when she was smaller. Especially on rainy days, as I usually had a hot bath waiting and fresh cookies. They were appreciative children and we had few problems.

In my childhood, I had few friends around and no brothers and sisters; only my dolls which were my friends. I loved music and would listen a lot to soft dreamy music and daydream I was a ballerina. I was able to have dancing and piano lessons. Being alone a lot, I read many books and learned to think things out for myself. When I thought back over the years, it was unbelievable that time could go by so fast.

Now here I was, after trying to make ends meet through these years, involved with the children's activities and being a busy homemaker, getting messages from the spirit world and opening up a whole new perspective about the meaning of life. I was feeling less interested in my domestic life now and more interested in finding out about more truths.

Dean was aware of the contacts coming through and the different incidents that occurred. Sometimes I felt he believed, then other times I strongly felt his doubts. I realized that was a natural reaction, especially since he came from a family of very reserved people. Dean seemed detached more out of being concerned with making a living in the moving business I thought, rather than from non-belief.

With the combination of his being away so much and when home, more withdrawn, it seemed like we were drifting more apart. Richard and Annette hardly saw him and when they did he was tired and uninterested.

Things came to a head when my father found out he had cancer. I knew Dean didn't have a lot of extra time, but I also felt he didn't have the inclination to be supportive. He either wasn't around to drive with me across the Bay Bridge to see my father at the hospital, or too tired to go.

During those many weeks, I drove across the bridge alone repeatedly. I had an hour and a half each way to think about things.

One Sunday I was returning from San Francisco after visiting with my failing father, Annette and Richard were with me. I was in a hurry to get back to Hayward and was driving faster than normal across the bridge and the freeway. As I got off the freeway and came into downtown Hayward, I slowed down for a stop light. My car lurched and the front right wheel rolled right off and darted across the next lane barely missing an oncoming car. My car spun around and landed partly on the curb! We were in shock but not hurt. As I was waiting for the tow truck to come, my mind thought back over the last hour. I visualized driving down those steep San Francisco hills from the hospital, barreling across the bridge and freeway, only minutes away from where my wheel blew off, to the only place it wouldn't have been disastrous. Then I remembered what we had been talking about in the car at the time. Richard was expressing his faith in God, thinking about his grandfather. Indeed... God was in charge.

My father did pass away shortly after that. My husband again was not around. In my disappointment I faced the fact of how unhappy I was with my marriage.

Perhaps this was on my mind subconsciously one morning as I sat at the kitchen table drinking a cup of coffee. I had a strong urge to pick up the pen. I was alone in the house, Richard and Annette were at school.

I looked down. My hand started moving. Scrawled out before me was, "The age of honesty has arrived, Tell your husband. You need to take separate paths. Free him, for continued growth... the time has come."

I looked down almost in disbelief. I had to admit I had thought about this... but actually doing it? What would Dean say? What would the children say? What would I do? I wasn't even working that much. My head started spinning.

About an hour later the phone rang. It was Yvette.

"Vikee, the strangest thing happened this morning, I got a message for you as I held my pen to begin writing my bills. It said, 'Tell Vikee the age of honesty has arrived'. Do you understand what that means?"

Yvette was gifted with psychic pushings and often received messages.

"Yvette! You would never guess. I received the very same message this morning!" I knew I had some decisions to make.

"Go forward with faith" my message had continued to say. As I pursued more information and getting together with Yvette, it was explained that we come onto earth with specific missions or assignments to fulfill. Again the term karma came up. My marriage with Dean was coming to the end of it's cycle. It was time to go on to another experience and lesson for our growth. My guide King William said there is a divine plan for every soul, and it is up to us to be open to it to not lose precious time. It is important we recognize our pushings, or thoughts to do certain things, even if it means changing our whole life. This takes courage and faith.

I thought perhaps if Dean had been more receptive it might have worked. Or, maybe it was just time for us to go our separate ways.

I picked a quiet time when I could have a talk with Richard and Annette. I knew their reaction would have a big bearing on what I decided.

I could hardly believe their reaction.

Richard began, "Mother, Annette and I understand more than you know. We see things and know you could be happier. We have even talked about it. We love you both and want you both happy. I know you have tried to cover up, but we know there are problems between you and Dad."

"He is so distant and impatient with us," Annette added, "maybe he's not happy either."

Richard went on, "Whatever you do, we will understand, we are behind you."

I felt so lucky that their reaction was so understanding. Tears came to my eyes as I realized how easy they made this decision for me... and how much I loved them.

CHAPTER FOUR

New Beginning

It had been six months since my guide told me the "age of honesty" had arrived. It was amazing how much my life had changed since that time. Dean and I had separated and the divorce was filed.

I thought back on Dean's reaction to our talk and my telling him how I felt. I am sure he was shocked; however, after thinking it over, he did not resist the idea. He was never one to show a lot of emotion. I had an inner feeling that he might have an interest elsewhere. I assured him there would be no problems in our settling everything fairly. It was agreed that he would be able to see Annette and Richard every other weekend unless they couldn't make it somehow. I told Dean with arrangements like this with the kids he would probably see them more than he had before, he had been home so little.

It did turn out that way. Dean began attending more baseball games Richard played in than ever before and the kids did make an attempt to go to the beach or events with him.

Why is it we almost have to feel we have lost something before we start appreciating it?

Dean began dating Lorna, my friend from high school, since she was divorced. He, Richard and Annette, and Lorna and her daughter would go to the beach often. I was glad, for I felt she would be good for Dean.

After nineteen years of marriage, I expected to go through more of a trauma than I did. When Dean left the house, I did cry, but more out of the sadness of an ending chapter in my life. I prayed he would be okay. I would always care for him and be concerned for his welfare.

I did not have a job when I filed for divorce, but I was getting assurance to keep the faith, from my guide, King William, or K.W. my nickname for him. He said if I would stay open I would be directed at the right time. I had been working part time for the school district and had in mind that before September I would take their test and apply for a school secretary opening.

Meanwhile, my mother coaxed me into coming to Los Angeles to visit before I started working full time. It worked out fine because Dean's parents, from Oklahoma, had invited Richard and Annette there for the summer.

During the time I was staying with my mother and step father Sandy, she tried to arrange for me to meet several men, but it was almost funny. It was like a "force" of some kind prevented it. Every time she arranged for me to meet someone, it never worked out that we met. We started laughing about it. But inwardly I felt I was not meant to live in that area.

A letter came from my lawyer saying I had to be back in town by August 15, to go to court. The weeks had flown, and it was time to return home. It was always special to be with my mother, we were like sisters. She was like a radiant light most of the time, but she did have her bad days and headaches. It was always hard to leave and say goodbye.

* * *

My moment in court was brief. There were no problems. Della went with me for support. It is always hard to say a final good bye to a big part of your life.

I had been home just over a week when I was guided to a job. My plan was to get caught up with duties around the house and shop for new clothes for school and work, and then look for a job. I found out the school district was not going to give their annual test after all, due to lack of openings.

Della's neighbor worked at a big company called Friden Calculator and mentioned that they were looking for a girl to work the front desk. Della encouraged me to go and interview. I did, and took the typing test. Three days later I was called to work.

Fall had begun, school was back in session. Dean agreed to let us stay in the house until Richard and Annette were out of school, then we would sell and divide our assets.

I thought more than once that maybe I had left my marriage too soon. I had less time now than ever. It was harder to make ends meet, and I did miss Dean living in the house.

It was harder to have the time to "communicate". I thought that maybe this was the time to get re-organized in my new life. I didn't go out much. I wasn't used to working full time and I needed my full evenings to do the things I had taken all day to do previously. My biggest pleasure was to soak in a bubble bath with a Ruth Montgomery book. Friends did invite me out for some occasions, but I had not met anyone special. In fact, I was too busy to think about social life that much.

A few months later I did meet an interesting man through my friend Jane. He had been married before, but a bachelor now for eight years. He was dating others so I did not feel any pressure.

Jason was good looking, tall, had side burns and was very slender. He had such a charming sense of humor I felt very comfortable with him. I couldn't remember when I laughed more. Our dates were fun and casual.

I don't know when I started to fall in love, but it happened. Jason was an Aquarius like myself, and full of spontaneous ideas. He took a sincere interest in both Richard and Annette. He was outgoing and they had a good rapport. Jason interested Richard in golf, which he loved. When Richard's music group was practicing at our house Jason would enjoy listening to him play on his guitar and saxophone. He would make helpful suggestions and also encouraged him to play the piano. Richard did spend more time creating new melodys and got a beginners book and taught himself to play, as he did with the guitar. It helped that Jason loved music as much as he did, giving them more common ground. He would "bop" with Annette as she loved dancing. We also went dancing often.

It was a wonderful adventure getting acquainted.

We did not get into the more serious subjects about life till later. I eventually mentioned the subject of life after death and how he felt about it. I was pleased that he was very easy and open to talk to. He was a definite believer that life goes on after death. He even shared with me that he felt his father's presence more than once after he died of cancer in his arms. He had been very close with his father. Jason did not like to dwell on these subjects however, so I didn't push.

I remember one evening he had invited me over to his apartment, by Lake Merritt. As I came in the front door and looked into his deep brown eyes, I had a sudden flashback. I knew we had lived together before in another lifetime. I saw him as a sea captain of a sailing vessel, and I told him so when I came in. He laughed at first, then said, "Well, anything's possible. Maybe that's why I have such a strong affiliation with having my own boat. I've always had some kind of boat, ever since I could first afford one." But then he went on to say, "That could be true, but isn't it enough right now just to get through today?"

I thought he had a very good point. Maybe he came into my life to keep me balanced. I gradually put aside the part of my life that involved the other dimensions and messages, for the time being.

CHAPTER FIVE

The Growing Years

After a lot of laughter, barbecues, baseball games (plus the ones that Richard played in), dance recitals, car and horse races, boating, and over one year later, I married Jason.
Prior to the marriage I had approached my son and daughter about their feelings to my marrying again. Annette was charmed with him as I was and was happy about having him as a stepfather. Richard liked Jason but preferred for me to take my time. I went to an old astrologer, Mr. Sterling, my friend Yvette swore by. He compared our birthday charts. We were both Aquarius's which usually isn't good he said, but we were an excellent match for each other. He also warned me to wait. He foresaw negative aspects in Jason's chart and said if he couldn't deal with the coming obstacles in a positive way it could lead to serious problems.
I had talked to Mr. Sterling about eight months after meeting Jason. But by the time a year had come around, I was

hopelessly in love and nothing would have mattered. Doesn't love conquer all? Dean had already remarried by then.

* * *

The months following our December marriage were wonderful. Jason worked at the oil refinery as a high climber in the bay area. Sometimes he worked up as high as two hundred feet. He often said that it would probably be the closest he would ever get to heaven! He had been a very social bachelor before our marriage, but once we married he preferred to be home as a family. I had hoped we could all be closer so Richard and Annette would have more family memories to look back on before they were on their own. I was disappointed that they had so many activities going on. We attended many, but mostly they were busy when a Sunday outing came around, or they were with their dad. They did go out with us occasionally in Jason's boat and learned to water ski.

Eight months after we were married, the accident happened. Jason was working eighty feet up. It was stormy that day. Because of an oil leak, making it dangerously greasy, and with the high winds, he and another man slipped and fell. They tried to break their fall on the way down. Fortunately neither man was killed, but they also never worked again.

During the next few years Jason was in countless hospitals with his injured spine and condition not improving. Finally the doctors agreed there was nothing they could do for him, for further surgery they feared could paralyze him. So he was told he would just have to "live" with his condition and pain the rest of his life.

Goodbye to golf and his active sports. But he wouldn't give up his boat... or hope.

* * *

It was difficult for Jason to be at home when the rest of us went out the door to work and school. He was used to working long hours and being very active. Everyone was busy but him. He was not used to being around teenagers. When Richard or Annette would come home from school and go into their rooms for privacy, he again felt left out, being over sensitive. He began to drink more. His pain was always there, difficult to live with, and he felt like an outsider. I tried to reassure him the kids were not doing anything different than they always had. We had our ups and downs as all adjusting families do, but we hung in there.

* * *

Months turned into years. Richard graduated from high school and went on to college. Annette graduated a year later and then attended the same college as her brother.

Richard moved to an apartment near the campus and also worked. Annette soon moved in with him. She went a year then decided to work full time.

Annette was a very pretty, dark-haired girl. Those deep brown eyes and loving smile soon won her young boss over, and in just a few months he proposed.

Doug was blonde, blue eyed, a quiet man with a disarming smile. They were married within the year.

In Annette's growing years she was very shy. She constantly was reading philosophical books looking for answers. She seemed to feel a sense of insecurity in her strong desire to please everyone. Richard and she were so close from the time they were toddlers it was hard to understand why she would have any insecure feelings. Now I realize that those very feelings can indeed go back to a previous lifetime and be carried forth. Hopefully, marriage would help make her feel more fulfilled.

Doug wanted to adventure and change jobs, so they moved north to Oregon. He began a trucking job and Annette worked at the college in Eugene.

One day my mother Patricia called with bad news. My stepfather Sandy, found out that it wasn't ulcers that had been upsetting his stomach. He finally went to the doctor for tests and found the prognosis terminal cancer, with six months to live. Richard always felt very close with his grandmother, so when she implored him to transfer and go to school in Los Angeles to be near them and help out, he didn't hesitate.

My mother tried very hard to put the desire into Sandy to not give up and try healing methods by spiritual means, but he turned into an angry man and accepted his verdict without a fight. In six months, he was gone.

Richard remained with his grandmother until the end of his school year and did everything he could to help her. We drove south to be with her also. But for the first time her spirit broke. She had loved her husband so much.

Her beautiful home meant nothing now, just an empty place without her Sandy. Through the years my mother had met countless health challenges, but now, her reason for living was gone. Her strength began to waiver.

I remembered back twenty-four years when Mayo Clinic had pronounced her doom, even though she was supposed to die, she kept her faith and determination. She defied medical prognosis and put her faith in God. But now, she was very tired, and on her twenty-third wedding anniversary, three months after her Sandy died, she slipped away from a heart attack.

Loving my mother so much, I felt guilty I had not been with her more. I had allowed my committing marriage to Jason keep me from visiting more. We did have our wonderful talks by telephone. I would miss that.

* * *

Richard did not pursue work in the computer field, his college major. He felt a more spiritual need than ever after losing two more of his small family. Since he had been dedicated to studies of the Eastern religions, having a deep respect for their simplicity and pureness of heart, he decided to journey north to a Buddhist retreat. Several weeks later, feeling more at peace, he went on to Eugene where his sister lived. Annette was now expecting a baby by Christmas and thrilled to have her dear brother near. She talked him into staying and he was soon connected with a music group.

Three weeks later Jason and I got a call from the hospital in Eugene. Annette was having problems and the doctor had to quickly take her baby caesarean. We tried to book an immediate flight to Oregon, but none were available till morning and it was very stormy. The storm had lessened by morning and we took the first flight out. A short while after we were airborne the pilot regretfully explained over the speaker that due to the overnight snow storm in Eugene and continuing snow, we would have to bypass there and land in Portland. I was heart sick. I started to cry.

Jason took my hand. "Vik, guess what! Your mother is on this plane! She just assured me we will land in Eugene," he smiled.

"Oh Jason, you're just trying to make me feel better." I remembered a few times Jason in the past had said, "I feel your mother around." He seemed to have those intuitive thoughts a lot.

"I mean it," he said. "She said to have faith. Remember, even when there seems no way, with faith a way will open."

I turned and looked at him, startled at the depth of his words. He may have been sipping on a drink, even with the plane bouncing around, but I saw his sincerity. I closed my eyes and prayed. I had to get to my daughter.

Forty minutes later as the plane neared the Eugene vicinity, the pilot spoke on the intercom. "Folks, we have a break, the way has cleared, it has stopped snowing and we will be able to make a landing after all. Please fasten your safety belts." Jason and I hugged. As we fastened our safety belts, and through my tears of gratitude I saw a big grin on Jason's face and a big knowing wink.

Doug and Richard were waiting at the airport. They drove us through the icy streets to the hospital. Annette's high fever made her face look so very flushed. But it began to come down that day. Our reunion was complete as we saw a smiling and radiant face holding a beautiful baby girl when the nurse gave her to her mother. I knew somewhere, my mother was smiling too...

CHAPTER SIX

Life In The Valley

That following summer Jason and I moved away from the congestion of the Bay Area to a slower paced little town in the valley. We found a cute little house by the river, about an hour inland from where we used to live. Richard based in Eugene and travelled with a local band to different towns in the Northwest.

After Jason and I had been settled a few months, I decided to work part time for Kelly Girl. It worked out all right for awhile, but gradually it turned out that when I got called for an assignment, Jason would come up with reasons why I shouldn't go. It was too foggy, or he needed my help at home. I would go along with what he wanted most of the time because I knew how much it meant to him that I do what he asked. His prior marriages were bitter disappointments. The past infidelities he had to deal with led him to be more suspicious and mistrusting in this marriage, especially since the accident. I tried to be understanding and didn't work that much.

We struggled on his disability pension and my occasional work. I did have some money in savings from my mother's house, but there were many medical bills. More money was being spent on alcohol than I wanted, but he said it helped dull the pain.

When I heard about some Inner Awareness classes in Stockton I really wanted to attend. I didn't go often however, because of Jason's moods. But through these classes it stressed the importance of being myself and fulfilling my own needs also. Alanon classes were suggested. I didn't know about Alanon before but found that they are a lifesaver to the one that lives with a drinker. Many mates think if they keep trying to get their spouse to quit drinking, they might eventually succeed. It is rarely so.

These important classes point out it is us that must change, our judgmental attitude and condemnation. We are not responsible for another's welfare or direction, no matter how much we love them and want to help them. It began to sink in that there wasn't anything I could do for my husband, only strengthen myself.

* * *

Doug, Annette's husband, would drop her off on a truck run south with little Nikki, about every six weeks. They were like a ray of sunshine when they came. Jason adored his little "Niki-nak", he called her. She would toddle after him down to the river to see the ducks. When she visited, they were inseparable, and of course he had to take her with him to town for a strawberry ice cream cone. We went out on the boat a lot when they were here, and Nikki loved the water. Jason was a wonderful grandfather. She called him "pa pa".

I heard from Richard about every two weeks. He was busy playing music from town to town. As the band travelled around he would try when he could to find a quiet place or a nearby church to meditate. He had a deep love for music, and it showed when he performed with his saxophone or guitar, but gradually, the atmosphere of the clubs began to bother him more and more.

Richard's spiritual pushings did not stop him from desiring companionship; however, it was hard to find the type of girl who would appreciate his philosophies. He did meet a girl very interested in Eastern teachings, and she invited him to go to yoga classes when he was in town. He enjoyed the relationship as they had many things in common, but his traveling kept him from settling down.

After Richard had been playing on the circuit with the band over a year, he became restless and knew he needed a change. I had missed him and our spiritual talks. I encouraged him to come to the valley, at least for awhile.

There was a little cottage on the back of our property. Richard regained much inner peace in the midst of such tranquility meditating there. It lead to getting a job in town at the health food store and eventually an apartment near. The owner took an immediate liking to him and was also into metaphysics. Richard was trained to manage the store plus he studied all his accredited material on the subject. Working in the store and helping people was a real pleasure for him and, understanding the importance of taking care of your body realizing the better the health, the clearer the inflow for higher thinking.

Richard's love for music was always there, and he eventually joined a local group playing music on weekends. It was through this group that he met Lynne. She was the singer of the band. She was a very attractive and intense young woman.

Jason, who loved music and dancing took me to hear them play a lot. I knew it hurt his back to dance but he would insist so I wouldn't argue. I tried to overlook his fast drinking when we were out as I realized he was trying to dull the pain. However, as the evening progressed, his personality would change.

I could see that Lynne was very attracted to Richard. She could hardly keep her eyes off him as she sang. I could feel the vibrations as they looked at each other. I found out she was a girl with many problems. Richard tried to be supportive to her and she leaned on him more and more, through the next weeks. I could feel his upset, for their friendship was turning into love as the weeks turned into months. The drawback was, she was married.

Richard tried to keep busy between working at the store, studying nutrition, and meditating. It became more difficult seeing Lynne at their practices. The intensity of their conversations grew. She was very unhappy in her marriage and said her husband was mean to her and her two girls. He felt very sorry for her but knew his hands were tied.

We talked one day and Richard confided to me how he felt about Lynne and the dismay of finding himself in such a futile situation. He did not want to fall in love in this hopeless way.

I told him if she really loved him, she would make a move and it would work out in time. It was better for now to keep out of it, to not to be the cause of their breakup. He sincerely prayed for help.

The answer to his prayers came through a phone call. A musician friend from Las Vegas remembered him and his talent. They needed a good sax player replacement and called to try and locate him.

Richard had been happy here, and cared about his job, but he knew his heart. It was time to leave.

* * *

Jason had started drinking more than ever. It was hard to try and forget the times he had been so unpleasant to Richard even though he did go to hear him play. I couldn't understand why he felt such a jealousy. It even stretched to my daughter's relationship with me. Annette and I talked a couple of times a week by phone as Doug was on the road all week. She needed a supportive lift, for Doug always seemed to be over-tired and withdrawn when he was home. Sometimes he lingered in the bar too long before he came home. I would point out to her the strain truckers went through coping with weather problems, especially over the mountains and how important it probably was for him to unwind in his own way.

It is hard to explain to the stepfather that the emotional support for your children does not stop just because they become adults. They need positive input. They need a good friend. Now I understand why Jason resented the attention I gave to anyone, even my friends because of his own insecurity, and this was intensified by alcohol.

I thought back how things were before we moved to the valley. Jason had had a bad liver attack making it critical he not drink. He knew it was a close call for him, so after recovering, he substituted soft drinks for vodka. I had been proud of him that he kept his strength. It was happier then.

Jason hadn't been drinking for three years when we moved out to the valley. Moving to a resort-like area with so many retired people around, and in responding to the warmth and over generous drinkers, it was hard not to be tempted to drink again, especially in that valley.

It seems that when you need the most to become strongest in your life, you can get caught up in your emotions and block that very help. The testing time is the hardest time to apply the principles you should. It is one thing to go to class or church and listen to uplifting statements for an hour, but the real test is applying them. Progress can be slow.

Jason was back to drinking.

CHAPTER SEVEN

Las Vegas

Going to Las Vegas was a good move. Not only did Richard get an opportunity to play with a known group there, but he was able to get into his spiritual studies with a clearer head. He missed Lynne a lot. It was one of the hardest things he had to do, move away from her. His heart was yearning to settle down. He hoped that if she loved him enough and if it was meant to be, she would find a way to come to him, free.

The Psychic Institute of Las Vegas took most of his extra time. When he wasn't working he stayed out of the clubs. He pursued metaphysical studies and lectures. He soon became accredited through a course in the science of Astrology.

Astrology has been misunderstood by many judgmental church goers or closed minded people that have not cared enough to investigate the real meaning of this art. It is an ancient law that is like a road map or guide through the lifetime of a soul. This science has been misinterpreted at times, or only part of it used, not bringing the true insight to help.

Thousands of years ago in Egypt and in the Orient this principle was followed as a way of life in making wise decisions. Marriages were carefully planned by it. One learns what to avoid and how to help yourself as you go through the life's lessons you karmically brought forth from the past.

Richard also studied more about healing methods. He learned true healing comes from within the soul or mind before it can have a permanent effect upon the body. Spiritual healing cleanses the heart of negative emotions that have festered within, thus creating a negative condition in the physical body. That is why doctors can only do so much, they only look at the outward body and results.

It was approaching Thanksgiving time and through my frequent contacts with my son, I knew how much he would like for us to all be together, as would I. His band was performing at the Tropicanna and I thought it would be fun to go. Jason's brother and family lived in Las Vegas and we had visited them frequently over the years. We had enjoyed seeing many shows there. I thought the trip would be good for all of us. Richard had always been on the road and never met them. Jason may have wanted to go, but because I wanted to go so much, and again because of his jealousy when he was drinking, he said we were not going. I tried to talk him into it, but the more I acted like it meant a lot to me, the more he became stubborn. I was heartsick.

The next time I was at an Alanon meeting I bought it up. It was suggested that drinkers often "game play" to keep their power, and that if I wanted to go, I should. It was time I started thinking of what made me happy.

That night I told Jason that I had decided to go on the trip Thanksgiving week with or without him. He became very upset so I did not mention it again, but I quietly made my plans. I called my friend Jane who lived in the Bay Area and made airplane reservations. Yes, she would take me to the airport and I could leave my car at her place. Jane was the one who introduced me to Jason many years ago, but she understood and was a good friend. I started to tell him I was going several times, but I knew he would make it so unpleasant for me that I would probably end up not going. I also knew his parents and sister would be around so he would not be alone for Thanksgiving. He also had many drinking friends and neighbors he spent much time with.

One morning a few days before Thanksgiving I slipped off and drove to the Bay Area. I left my car there and Jane took me to the airport as planned. I had left Jason a note. I was upset to my stomach as I hated to leave this way, but I just couldn't face his anger. I hadn't stood up to him this firmly before. It became the turning point in our marriage.

When Jason found my note and realized I really had left without him, he was furious. Then after a couple of days he felt dejected and hurt. After three days he called Richard's apartment in Las Vegas demanding I come home. When I told him I had actually gotten ill over this and had been down he didn't buy it. Then he said he would quit drinking if I came home.

He said, "If you don't get yourself back here now then you can just stay there."

I answered, "You know, if you are really sincere about quitting drinking, you don't need me to help you stop. You could make an appointment and see the doctor, you can call AA."

"I need you now," he retorted.

"I need to stay here awhile. You chose not to come, remember? You have your family there for Thanksgiving. I won't even contact your brother." I was having a hard time not feeling guilty.

Through Jason's fury he declared, "You stay there and do your thing. I will do mine! Goodbye!" He hung up.

Again the upset, I ran into the bathroom. Should I go back? He had said these things to me before when I had made an occasional trip to Oregon to visit Annette in the past. I put my head back on the chair, tears rolling down my face.

I ended up staying two weeks. I needed that time for me. While Richard was working I began to totally relax, mentally and physically, sunning around the pool. The sun lightened up my blonde hair even more. I attended the Unity church and spent a lot of time at the Psychic Institute for counselling, lectures and readings. Richard and I had many interesting talks. He was trying to build a new life. We prayed together. I knew I had to realign my life also. I had gotten too far away from thinking spiritually due to my emotions.

* * *

After I had come to Las Vegas to visit Richard, he related a strange experience he recently had. More than once he felt the presence of a Being from out in space. It seemed to be beckoning him out to the desert. He dreamed about it several times. He told a friend Angela about it. She didn't think he should go when he wanted to take a drive out there at night. Eventually the pushing went away. He hadn't been apprehensive about it, but he didn't end up going. Then he got busier and he put it out of his mind. Later on, he was contacted again by this being, and did have communication with him.

* * *

The two weeks had flown by. I loved the town, the fantastic buffets the clubs had, the night lights glittering up and down the strip. It was exciting for me to hear Richard play music in this glamorous city. But I knew I had better get back home.

I had been praying for Jason. I found an inner peace being away and re-evaluated many things. I knew I would do everything possible to try and help him, this time on a much more spiritual basis. I really wanted to have things work out in my marriage. These two weeks helped me become renewed and stronger. I would go home anticipating a better life, hopefully with my husband.

As my plane neared the airport I felt more exhilarated than I had in along time.

CHAPTER EIGHT

The Return

My return home was not what I had hoped for. Emma, Jason's sister warned me the evening I got back. I stopped by there first on the way home, thinking Jason might be there. She said he had been drinking more than ever. He was still very angry with me, not only for leaving, but staying away as long as I did. I hoped she was exaggerating. But she was not.

My dear husband did not come stumbling home until five in the morning, and he was filled with hostility. I was heartsick. He wanted nothing to do with me.

In the days following, he would get up and start drinking, then leave the house. He would not return until very late, and very intoxicated. I tried to talk to him about how important the trip was to me to get a new insight on my life. He was not interested in anything I had to say. He wanted to punish me for my leaving. He said he didn't need me anymore, he had found someone else who understood and was there for him. I was shocked and hurt.

I tested him and asked, "Please be honest with me. Is there really someone else? If you mean that, then I will leave."

He avoided an answer. "Do what you want. It makes no difference." he went on.

I wanted to stall for time. I tried to pass it off, and see how things would be by New Year's, our special time, three weeks away. Our wedding anniversary came and he didn't even come home. I knew something had to give soon. I wouldn't let myself dwell on another woman. All of our fourteen years Jason had prided himself on his faithfulness. But he wasn't in such bad mental and physical state as he was in now.

I had come home to a real test. I tried to keep my faith.

One night a week later, with nothing improved, Jason started out the door again. I asked him if he would please stay home. He went out the door, hostile as ever.

Heartsick I sat down and cried, as he pulled out of the driveway. I don't know how long I just sat there. I got up and began to walk down to the river. I loved to sit and stare into the water. I went there every day, trying to feel more positive about everything. But this evening as I looked out over the water I began to carefully remember everything that I had so joyously absorbed while I was in Las Vegas.

Had I let my faith waiver? Did I only love Jason if he was the way I wanted him, or could I love him unconditionally? If I loved him no matter what, then I must reflect that to him. In my heart I had known it wouldn't be easy before I ever returned home, so why should I let this big challenge get me down? I closed my eyes and listened within. An inner voice was saying, "Remember your truths. You will be directed." It was like a door opened to me. I had been trying so hard to have things work out, I found myself realizing that I let the problem overtake me. I allowed myself be in a web of emotion rather than totally turning my plight over to divine love and wisdom... then letting it go.

Out of my despair, I felt a strong surge of love and understanding for my husband. Even though he acted hostile, I knew how very insecure he really was. I could see that now.

It must have started when he went into the army at seventeen. Then the unexpected Korean outbreak came only months later while he was stationed in Honolulu with little training behind him. From fun times to terror at the front lines. After a year and a half of seeing death and horror all around him, and constantly praying to live, he returned home and was supposed to be normal. He married too soon only to later find his wife unfaithful with his best friend. Then a divorce he didn't want, a baby girl he couldn't see anymore, then another marriage on rebound that turn to disaster as his wife's family never acknowledged him since he had been married before and they were devout Catholics. I met Jason eight years after that, already drinking more than he should. I could see why it was so important to him to know he could count on me, and my love.

Perhaps his feeling at times of jealousy of my children stemmed because his were taken out of his life with no desire to see him; whereas I had such closeness through the years with mine.

There is always a reason why we are led to the destructive path we take. It is too easy for the one on the outside to try and change the other person, and too quick to judge. I realized how much physical and emotional pain Jason was struggling with over these years and how inadequate he really felt by not working, in spite of the fact he was very resourceful around the house and helpful to friends and neighbors working on projects.

How could I relate my feelings of love and compassion to him? Where would he be? I called a buddy of his he often drank with hoping he was there instead of with a woman. He was there.

"Jason..." I was trying to find the right words to lure him back home. "I have really missed you. Would you... please come home? I really love you... come home and I will show you how much." He was silent.

"Jason... will you come?"

After more hesitation he finally said softly, "Yes."

My heart surged with excitement. I wanted to look desirable to him. I raced to get ready.

By the time I had stepped out of the shower, ran the brush through my hair and added more lipstick and perfume, I heard the front door open.

I walked into the living room wearing the negligee he had bought me on my last birthday. It was a very cold December night. He was standing in front of the wall heater, his bulky Levi jacket still on. He looked at me. He was handsome, desirable. It was a very special moment for both of us. I will never forget that scene as long as I live. I walked over to him and we embraced. There were tears in his eyes as he said, "I love you Vikee... please forgive me." His kiss penetrated into my soul.

I whispered in his ear, "There is nothing to forgive..." That evening and many to follow were very magical for us.

CHAPTER NINE

Goodbye, Jason

"To be reborn, first you must die..."

From The Case for Reincarnation *by Joe Fisher*

If we could only stop time when we feel the happiest. Unfortunately, the growing intensity of Jason's pain led him back to drinking excessively again. I begged him to go back to the doctor for help but he felt it was futile. I prayed for him. I tried to persuade him to at least let me read healing and uplifting passages from inspirational books, but he would shut me out.

By Christmas I could see the writing on the wall. It was sad. Even though we loved each other, more than ever now, he could not seem to help himself from his path of self-destruction. Love did not seem enough.

* * *

Then it happened. The morning of New Year's eve, while in the kitchen I heard a gagging sound from the bedroom. I ran in and saw blood pouring out of Jason's nose and mouth. There was fright, in his eyes as he gasped, "You'd better get a doctor!"

For a moment I was so emotional my mind froze. Then I pulled myself together and called an ambulance. By the time they arrived Jason had thrown up two pan fulls of blood, I quietly cried all the way to the hospital as I followed the ambulance.

After what seemed like an eternity, they stabilized him after two blood transfusions. He survived, but it was touch and go. Time was lost as the hours melted together and I realized I was there all day and evening. The night nurse insisted I go home and get some rest, as Jason was heavily drugged by then.

As I was driving home from the hospital, all of a sudden I heard horns honking around me on the streets. It was midnight, New Year's eve! I started to cry... our special night. I felt dread for this new uncertain year.

Every month for the next nine months the doctors were amazed Jason lived as long as he did. His liver was damaged beyond repair. His esophagus had become so irritated and inflamed from constant alcohol it had caused internal bleeding from over a long period of time. It also appeared he had pneumonia, but he wasn't stable enough for further probing. Weeks later they finally determined that the condition in his lungs was in fact, tuberculosis. No wonder I couldn't get him to go back to the doctor. He must have had an inner knowing just how bad off he really was and tried to cover it with alcohol.

I lived from day to day, back and forth to the hospital, not knowing how long. The specialist tapped Jason's stomach frequently to relieve the fluid buildup, but it left him weak. His doctor finally wanted him taken to University of California Hospital in San Francisco to see if there was anything they might do to prolong his life. I agreed to anything that might make a turn for the good. It took two hours to drive there, including crossing the bay bridge. Always so much traffic. Then it was so hard to say goodbye when I had to go back home.

The doctors considered putting a shunt, like a tube in the abdominal area for drainage to relieve the pressure. Later they decided against it thinking he might not survive the procedure.

After two weeks of trying to rebuild his strength on supplements and medication Jason wanted to go home. The doctors said there was nothing more they could do, and agreed.

Annette and Nikki had come from Oregon to be with us. Nikki, now three, was like a precious little nurse. She brought the smile to her papa Jason's face as she patted and kissed him. When he was taken back to the hospital we even managed to slip her in his hospital room for some extra hugs and attention. Many times when we were back home and it was dark we would go up on our sundeck and look up at the stars. We would say, "Star bright, star light, first star I see..." Nikki wishing her papa would get better... and I praying he would be out of pain.

Richard called from New York. His Las Vegas band had just returned from an engagement in Aruba in the south Carribean. We had been keeping in touch. I told him I didn't think Jason had many more days. Richard had already made previous arrangements for a fill-in when the time came. I told him there was nothing he could do, but he flew in two days later.

Jason was in and out of a semi-coma all week. What made it hard was seeing him restrained and moaning in pain when he wasn't staring into space. His mother and stepfather had come from out of town and were staying with Emma. Jason's brother and wife had flown in from Las Vegas. And, after all these years, his daughter from his first marriage had come. It was hard to know whether he was aware of her presence or not. Sad, for he had been in despair so many times in the past because she didn't want to see him.

When Richard arrived, I was with Jason. As he took his hand and spoke to Jason he opened his eyes in recognition.

Richard talked of old times when he was a teenager and nearly wrecked Jason's car learning to drive. Although he couldn't speak, tears came from his eyes. Richard embraced him as he leaned over him, whispering into his ear. He looked more peaceful as he closed his eyes.

Jason's life on earth ended on a warm September night. It was late, everyone had left. I sat next to his bed. I could hear the sprinklers going outside and looked out the window. The moon was bright and full. He did not seem conscious. I held his hand. Then something strange happened. It was like an embodied mist rose up from him. Though no words were spoken I knew he was trying to relate to me in spirit.

"Go home, Vikee. I am okay now. You see I'm not in that old body. It's okay. I want you to go home."

He was still breathing, his body warm, I thought I was dreaming.

It startled me so, I jumped up. He was somehow imparting to me to leave. I was exhausted. The stress of "not knowing when" and absorbing the situation so intensely these last months had taken its toll. I reluctantly went home to rest.

I had been home about an hour when the hospital called. Jason had passed over. I became very upset that I hadn't been with him. Then I realized. This is the way he wanted it.

It was three o'clock in the morning when we got to the hospital again. Annette came with me. Richard stayed home with Nikki and prayed for Jason's passing.

Jason's parents and sister were already there. We all embraced over the final goodbyes with many tears. After they left, Annette and I just sat there for awhile, holding on to Jason's hands. I knew I would not see his face again, or his pain wracked body, for the Neptune Society would be picking him up soon, to later have him cremated. I had made a promise that when the time came I would scatter his ashes into the river he used to fish in as a little boy, with his grandfather. The same river we lived near.

* * *

Two weeks later just Richard, Annette, Nikki, Emma and I took Jay's ashes, went by his favorite spot up river and had our quiet little service. We got up on the old train bridge that overlooked his beloved river, where we had taken our boat so many times.

As I tossed out the ashes from the bridge, Richard chanted mantras in sanskrit, the Buddhist prayers for eternal life. Like magic the ashes swooped up and out... then floated down onto the water.

"Papa's watching us!" cried Nikki, looking up. "I love you!" her little voice said. She knew he was near. As she threw a kiss up to the sky, I felt my anguished heart twist in half.

I knew she would never forget her "papa".

CHAPTER TEN

The Messages Begin Again

After the change called death takes place, do we meet those gone before?

MAN IS NOT ANNIHILATED, NOR DOES HE LOSE HIS IDENTITY BY PASSING THROUGH THE BELIEF CALLED DEATH. AFTER THE MOMENTARY BELIEF OF DYING PASSES FROM MORTAL MIND, THIS MIND IS STILL IN A CONSCIOUS STATE OF EXISTENCE... TO AWAKEN WITH THOUGHTS, AND BEING, AS MATERIAL AS BEFORE. WHEN WE SHALL HAVE COME UPON THE SAME PLACE OF CONSCIOUS EXISTENCE WITH THOSE GONE BEFORE, THEN WE SHALL BE ABLE TO COMMUNICATE WITH AND TO RECOGNIZE THEM."

From Miscellaneous Writings, 1883-1896, by Mary Baker Eddy

There is unbearable pain in ending a very emotional part of your life. Then the numbness sets in. The weeks following due to the mental strain of the months, were mostly adjusting and resting. I was so exhausted that I found it hard to even get out of bed. I spent much time in self guilt, and thinking "why didn't I do this?" or "if only I had done that, things might have been different." Then eventually realized that I did the best that I could at the time.

I was truly blessed to have had my son and daughter with me. Richard had planned to stay with me as long as he felt I needed him. He helped financially, around the house, and gave much loving support. He was able to get his job back at the health food store, which was a break. Some time later he began playing music on weekends with a local group.

Annette never returned to Oregon to live. Was the timing accidental? During the weeks she and Nikki were in California with Jason and me, the telephone conversations with Doug became more distant. At first he was impatient about her coming back. She tried to explain she could not return with Jason's death so close. Doug was used to not having inconveniences at home. There were more arguments and misunderstandings with each call. I encouraged Annette to return home but she would not think of leaving at this point and was upset at Doug for not understanding. She and Jason had many special talks through the years and he was always there when she needed someone.

It turned out Doug told her to stay in California, he wanted his freedom. After Jason died I tried to get her to go back and try and patch things up, but he had hurt her too many times. The marriage was over. This kind of loss is just as traumatic as loss through death.

* * *

During Jason's illness I had tried to get some written messages about him. Most of them said to keep my faith and to release him. When I asked when he would leave me, I never got a definite answer. I see now it was better not to know. Now that he had left, I wanted desperately to contact him. I believed I could astral travel and be with him at night in dreams, but I rarely could remember my dreams. Emotions block our inflow.

The night before our wedding anniversary I could hardly sleep, so many thoughts going through mind. It would have been fifteen years. I knew the next day would be a tough one to get through. Well, I made it past Thanksgiving, didn't I? My last Thanksgiving was spent in Las Vegas without him.

I always left our stereo on softly at night. I finally drifted off to sleep remembering how special all of our anniversaries had been, with champagne or special wine. He always had brought me roses and we would enjoy a fancy dinner.

I awoke to music drifting in my ears. The stereo was playing, "The Days of Wine and Roses"! A chill ran through me as I woke with a start. That couldn't have been a coincidence. What a way to wake up on my anniversary. I knew my Jason was around. I jumped out of bed in excitement and yelled at Annette as I grabbed a pen and paper. She was excited with me.

A message from Jason:
I asked, "Is this really you, here, on our anniversary?"
"Yes" came through on paper. "am getting help."
"Are you doing okay? Are you happy?"
"No. Because of mistakes on earth. Sad for that."
"Do you have resentments still?" I asked.
"No. Only sorrow for mistakes..."
"Jason. I love you. We both made mistakes."
"I need more rest..."
"Yes. I understand. Have you seen your father?"
"Yes. And your mother... many."
"Is it hard to come through?"
"Yes. Too soon."
"Am I doing okay?" I asked.
"No. You need to release more... no need for guilt."
"I am trying. Haven't we met in dreams?"

"Yes."
"Why can't I remember?"
"Blocked."
"What can I do to remember?"
"Pray. Your prayers are helping me. They helped me come over in peace... have to go. Happy anniversary my love, I am with you... Jason."

I was thrilled. My anniversary could not be sad now. Love cannot be separated.

* * *

Weeks later, I was able to get more messages through, but not often. I began to remember my dreams more. One night, in a dream, Jason and I were walking together along the river contentedly. It felt so real. The more I prayed and meditated the more inflow I received.

One day after meditation I picked up the pen and asked my guide, K.W., about Jason's frame of mind before his death. A couple of times he had seen something we couldn't see and he looked frightened.

From K.W.: *"Jason could see the other dimension before he actually passed over, when he was in a semi-conscious state. He did see some unpleasant things that were a part of his inner fears and hostilities. Because of your strong love and prayers, when he actually did pass over he did not carry as much fear or resentment. He did pass over in peace. He was greeted with loving friends, relatives and helpers before he went to a sleep state to recuperate from his illness. When you thought of him, he awoke momentarily and came."*

* * *

How important for us to send love and prayers. I had read many times that by sending out this loving light, it attracts higher powers to reach them. If I hadn't been so emotional when he was alive, I might have been a better example of faith.

* * *

Not long after that another message came through by pen from Jason. He had felt my guilts and regrets:

"You had to do what you felt, just as I did. I see you are dwelling too much on what could have been. We both made mistakes, Vik, but to help each other we must go forward. I want to. Do not keep clinging to the past. I was sick in mind as well as body, or I would have appreciated you and your kids so much more. Maybe next time around we can give more. I am sorry for the many hurts. Knowing we can communicate has helped me progress more than I ever would have. This has made the adjustment so much easier. I love you now, and forever, Vik. We love many times in eternity, but you are my special one. I will see you again. Love, Jason,"

What more could a widow ask for?

* * *

I began to see the importance of thinking of my husband and his death in the right way. My attitude lifted into more peace rather than a sense of loss or sadness. I knew he was not dead. He was around when I needed him. I could see how it was a hindrance to him to keep clinging. This made it easier to release him so he could progress.

It was sad I couldn't share this with most of my friends and others, as so many would not be open, or even try to understand. Why is it people would rather criticize something than to be open for new truths? This would have to change someday, for it could lift up the vibration of the whole world. By eliminating grief, it would eliminate much negativity.

* * *

During the day I took care of Nikki while Annette worked. I would take her to the library to their story hour every week and during that time ponder over different spiritually uplifting books. I was happy to see there were so many that backed up my own truths, some written centuries ago.

One day I checked out a book called *No Goodbyes – a Trip into the Beyond* by Adela Rogers St. John. I knew she was a well known and respected journalist. It seemed she had no previous beliefs about the beyond until after her son and then her husband died. The famous psychic Ruth Garratt contacted her from England with a message from her deceased son. This experience led her into further investigation. Going from the Ouija board, then automatic writing led to direct method of contact, into the astral plane. This method began with lying down, blindfolded, and prayer.

I thought back to Richard's earlier ability to change places with his grandfather and wondered what could now transpire. After Richard came home from work that evening I asked him if he would be willing to try once again to make a direct spiritual contact into the next realm, and possibly reach Jason. He agreed. So, after all these years, we were once again going to tap into the "other" realm.

* * *

Richard reclined on the sofa, blindfolded. I held his wrist, as mentioned in the book, and "circled" him in the light. As one's thoughts go out to the universe it is very important to be totally positive, raising the vibration to a higher level. As Richard lay reclined, many thoughts flashed through my mind. Could I get a direct message from Jason? Would my father still come through after all these years?

It seemed like a long time before his lips began to move. He said, "I see your mother. She says we worry too much. She sends her love."

It had been several years since my mother had passed away. How exciting to feel her close again! I talked to her, through

Richard. Then I asked her about her husband Sandy, who passed away months before her.

"*Sandy is sleeping mostly,*" she answered.

I asked, "Can you communicate with him now?"

My mother replied through Richard, *"No, not till he awakens more."* Then my mother left.

I asked, "Is Jason doing better?" asking Richard direct.

"Yes. I see him. He is thankful for prayers. Wants to help... is helping..... He is gone!"

How wonderful to feel the closeness of someone you love. Then I asked about my father.

"I see him. He looks young. They all send love to us."

That was the first attempt to tap over into the next plane. Richard was able to alter his consciousness and "see" whoever came to him. He could describe everything he saw clearly. He wished he was an artist so he could sketch what he saw. Regardless of what anyone else might think, I knew his inner vision was real. The continuance of life beyond the grave is shocking to some, unbelievable to others, and overwhelmingly wonderful for others, to know they can still keep in contact.

* * *

The days following became very exciting as Richard and I continued with the contacts. He was the receiver and I would write down everything that came through. Relatives and close friends that had passed over, gradually started coming to him with messages and concerns. What amazed him was the entity came to him "as they wished to appear", usually younger.

I was very happy when my father came forward. I asked, "Have you been around us through these years, daddy?"

He answered, *"Yes Donna (he still called me Donna) I have been around."*

"Did our attempt at communication through the years to you help you advance after you passed away?"

"Yes. Very much so. The inspiration I needed to progress."

"How wonderful," I exclaimed,

"There are many who want to come through. I will return again. Love, Dad."

* * *

After hesitation, Richard said, "I see a man in his fifties, grey hair and sideburns, moustache, very good looking. I do not know him." Richard's eyes were closed, but even with the darkness forms and faces appeared vividly.

"The man says you know him as RX. Do you know a RX?"

"RX! That's my guide that has been coming through from my automatic writing! I wish I could see him."

I greeted RX and asked him about Jason. He replied, *"He is not ready for this yet, it takes more preparation. You must release him more. Release as we do here, for true peace. Let each one find his own path, be helpful when needed, but stay clear of other's tracks. You must go forward now, so you can prepare for times to come."*

* * *

After a moment Richard went on, "Here comes another. I do not know him either. He says he is called King William. He is bald, around in his forties. He wants to say something."

I leaned forward expectantly. He was also my guide and Della's.

"It is good to get in touch with you. You are getting a lot of help. More than you can imagine. You must continue now to communicate, meditate and evaluate. Your husband loves you like we all do. You must understand. Love is different here. It is right. Not based so much on attachment and desire as there. Tell Della hello. Think of me and I will send you light."

It was fascinating to know that Richard was not aware of these entities as he had been on the road so much playing music. This was something quietly shared by Della and I.

The next day I unexpectedly received a check of $4,000, with an explanation from the insurance company that they had come across this mistake of still owing me after the home loan had been paid off due to Jason's death. An answer to a prayer! The house paid off and money besides!

That night when Richard and I tried to make a contact, my father came through with the following message:

"Donna. How did you like your present today from us? You know me, the CPA. Enjoy it. We are proud of your positive mind and great faith. We admire you for your efforts to bridge over to all of us. I hope you keep it up, for all of our sakes. You have enriched my life... and my soul. Today was the beginning of many things that will fall into your lap during your life there. You are so special to me and your mother. We are sorry we were not more loving when you were little... but time will make it up to you. Enjoy the money and think of us. Love, Dad."

Wow! What a beautiful message and what a blessing. I was amazed at the thought that my father and "friends" really could have had something to do with correcting the oversight. He had been a brilliant accountant. I thought of the Bible phrase, "All things are possible to them that believe..."

Another day my dear grandmother Lewis came through who had helped me some years back to save my mother's life.

"I am coming soon to your side, Donna." (what she always called me). *"I have had a nice rest here. It is time to get on with things. Life is a continual cyclic experience. Birth and death are much of the same."*

I was so happy for this communication. I always felt close to her. With her new rebirth coming, she would be in an age of much to happen according to predictions.

I asked her, "Is earth really going to be shook up all around the year 2000?" I had read this more than once.

"It depends on all of you. Please keep on praying for the world. This is very important to help its vibrations. And, please remember me in prayer for my soon coming incarnation to be a fruitful one," she added.

"Grandmother, will I know who you will be?"

"No, my dear. I will be in another country. Do you remember how much I always loved flowers? When you pick a flower, please think of me..."

I knew I always would.

* * *

Richard and I were very excited about the breakthroughs. We tried to receive messages at least three times a week when possible. At first the messages came mostly from relatives and guides, RX and KW.

One evening RX related: *"You must continue to do this work for the good of all. We will help you with material matters. We are sending helpers to you all the time, on both sides."*

I remembered Richard's description of him and a thought came to me: "RX, have we ever been together in another lifetime?"

"Yes. I hope you like mustaches."

I laughed with delight.

"Maybe that's why I always was attracted to them. Could you tell me about a past life that we were together?" I asked.

"Yes. Another time. Goodbye for now." He was gone.

* * *

When my mother, Patricia, came through I asked her, "Mother, have you gone to a school for further training there on the other side?"

She answered, *"Oh boy, did I. But not right away. Time is not the same here. You can't equate it to earth time at all. It feels like I have been here one hundred years instead of just a few."*

I have a painting hanging in my living room of my lovely mother. She had it done for her husband, Sandy, years ago. In the painting she was in her late 30's, with black hair, blue sensuous eyes. Her black lace gown fell off her shoulders, looking very seductive. As she became older she lightened her hair color and was blonde, the last ten years of her life. But no matter how old she became, her face stayed beautiful without a blemish on it. She was sixty-two when she went across to the other side.

"What color is your hair now, mother?" I questioned.

"Any color you like. You pick, ha ha," she added. *"Thought creates the reality. It is all up to us. Great, eh?"* The thought came to me that we create our own reality here on earth, too, in so many ways. For our truths are what is real to us.

Another time I asked her, "Can you see Sandy whenever you want?"

"Yes. Each soul has their own set of responsibilities. You learn, re-evaluate and prepare for the next incarnation. Hard to explain. You can be with anyone you want when you think of them. They are also working and resting."

* * *

One evening, KW related through Richard, *"Judge not others, because most of you are confused. Only a few are not. Confusion is not natural, so remember to be compassionate for the others because they are not in their natural state of being. Be patient with yourself and others. Do not depend on happiness outside of yourself. As long as you remain confused, happiness can only be in small spurts. The most important thing you can do is to strengthen your spiritual nature, and Truth will follow."*

* * *

Just before Easter, an angel-like presence appeared with the following message: *"The most important lesson in life is to have a positive outlook always. Faith and positive thoughts bring the real happiness. Love others, serve others, and walk your path. Each must do his own work. Do not worry about anything. If only you knew how much is already planned for you, you would see that to worry is indeed a waste. So, be open so you can let your path unfold unto itself. Remember the more you can accomplish the sooner you will be one with God. Remember, we* are all in One, so have patience and compassion for all. Do not let another take you away from your path."

* * *

Another time: *"The world is going through a big change now and in the next few years. Our advice to you is to live as simply as possible. Eliminate possessions not needed so you can focus more on the Truth. Spend time alone each day in silence... and meditate. It is better not to have desires of this world because everything is unimportant on that plane. It is a waste of time to accumulate riches. The Kingdom of God is the real wealth, for once attained, it is never lost. You are truly loved. Signed, Your friends from Above."*

* * *

Richard and I realized we were going to get messages now, from many levels, not only those in the dimension close to us, but higher levels. He found it unnecessary to use a blindfold any longer. He now was getting messages from entities of different backgrounds and at different time periods from the past.

* * *

One night Richard described a young, pretty woman with long, dark hair wanting to approach, but hesitating. He did not know who she was. Two nights later she reappeared to him.

She spoke. *"My name is Eve, Evelyn."* She was talking through Richard to me! *"I was your last sister. We came out west together..."* she broke off. Richard said, she couldn't go on. He perceived her as very resentful of me, and apparently had been for a long time. He saw a connection between her, RX and me! He saw RX in the background.

I called for RX and asked him about Eve. He came forward.

"It is not for me to explain. This is something Eve will do when she can. This was progress for her to speak to you. Pray

for her and send the white light to her. She is your sister from before, so let her tell you. You will know more soon. Love, RX."

I was fascinated with this new event. My impatience for answers led me to try to find out more with my automatic writing. The next day I relaxed and picked up my pen, after meditation. I waited. Suddenly I did feel a woman's presence. The following words came through:

"You and I went west in a wagon train, and RX was with us. His name then was Matt. Matt was in love with me until you interfered. When we reached Oregon you left with him. I hated you for it."

I was stunned. I wanted to find out more. I asked about our mother.

"Our mother died before we went out west. Our father was with us."

I asked, "Did you ever marry later?"

"Yes, but I never loved him. I loved Matt," my pen scrawled out. A sudden thrust of guilt overtook me. How sad.

In my mind I asked Eve, "Did we ever see each other after that?"

"No. You had a child. A girl. I never had any children. I wanted them." I felt Eve leave. My pen dropped, I called out for her, but she was gone. Could all this really be true?

* * *

That night through Richard I called to RX. When he appeared I asked, "RX, is your past name Matt? Were you aware of the message I received from Eve today?"

"Yes," he answered. *"Now that you know who I am, I will call you Martha, for that is your name to me."*

"Is it true I came out west in a covered wagon and then ran off with you?"

"Yes, it is. Now you know why I have a special interest in your welfare."

"I am flabbergasted. What else happened, Matt?"

"That is enough to tell for now," he related.

Then Richard said, "Eve is here. She wants to speak."

She began, *"He was promised to me. You took him away from me. I was jealous and resentful. I wish to leave now... Eve."*

"Don't go", I implored. I wanted to tell her how sorry I was that she had been hurt. But she was gone. Then Matt came. *"Martha, we were all so young. I have also suffered. I have had to watch you be unhappy for many years, and not be able to be with you in your life. There is a lesson here for all."*

"Then all of my earlier messages by pen were true?"

"Yes, Martha."

"Can't you tell me more?" I asked.

"You will know more soon. Have to go... Matt."

* * *

I had a lot to think about. I had believed in the existence of past lives ever since I started following the writings of Edgar Cayce, the sleeping prophet. It had always made sense to me.

His fame began in the early 1900's. Many came to discredit him but went away believing. City librarys and book stores have many books written about him. His son, Hugh Lynn Cayce established a center in Virginia Beach called the Association of Research and Enlightenment where thousands of files and recordings are kept of accounts of reincarnation and the effect on this lifetime. In his sleep state, Edgar Cayce was able to bring forth information that helped everyone who came to him for advice or healing. He informed them of methods of healing based on natural means from the earth. It logically showed why rebirth is a natural part of the cycle of life and necessary to the growth of the evolving soul.

The belief of reincarnation has been going on for thousands of years, in the Orient, Egypt and many other parts of the world, long before our country was even discovered. If one reads and ponders on these truths, it will unfold its logic, that life, like the seasons is a continuous cycle. As one learns more in each grade in school, so man learns in each life time, often by trial and error by his many mistakes. The Bible says, "what ye sow, then also ye reap". This is the law of cause and effect in how we handle our lives, also called karma by Eastern religions.

I remembered many months ago watching Shirley MacLaine on the Donahue talk show regarding her book *Out on a Limb* where she revealed how she came into these same truths. I was so pleased with everything she said. She went on to say these truths have always been, but man had blocked himself from becoming aware of them, until his inner and higher self wanted to become aware. Later in her next book, *Dancing in the Light*, even more truths of the beyond and reincarnation came out. Through Kevin Ryerson, a channeler, she learned much more from the other dimension.

It was gratifying to hear of other channelers and trance mediums that were bringing forth spiritual information, confirming life "on the other side", thus bringing forth the naturalness of this phenomenon.

Another time when Shirley MacLaine was being interviewed on television by Gary Collins, I was quick enough to get it on tape for future reference. I was pleased the way she presented her views on karma and past lifetimes, and grateful someone so famous would be speaking up. She verified that the universal law brings back into your life the unfinished problems or emotions that needed to be corrected and then released.

* * *

One day RX said, *"My dear, the truth is that there are so many of us that want to communicate with you to assure you there is no real death, but a continuation of the life cycle. Because more are becoming open, communication will be easier than ever before. As long as you stay open, you will be forewarned of any disasters. Remember, you will not find Truth in crowds. Love, RX/Matt."*

Richard found that the more time he spent in meditation and prayer prior to tapping in, the clearer the message and the less his body would be tired afterwards. Sometimes, however, as we waited, and often with candles burning, no one would appear to him. Sometimes interference from outside, or sudden noises would break the communication after it began. We also realized that our contacts would not always come if they were busy elsewhere. Then we would look over and discuss what information we had already accumulated from the tapes or written down. Richard usually was not aware what was said during contact although he was aware of who appeared. From his altered state he could describe details of what each one was wearing, the expressions on their faces, and emotions emanating from them.

Annette was with us a lot of the time and shared our joys and excitement of communication. My mother always came through when Annette was there. When she appeared there was humor in her personality, same as always. It had been hard for Annette to get over her husband. My mother said she was looking around for a companion for her. She was always a comfort to her when she had her down moments.

"You must believe. I love you all, and little Nikki." she said. *"Do not stay unhappy. Remember how much help you have up here. Don't forget us when you need us the most. You will be surprised in the good to come if you keep your faith..."*

Annette did start seeing a fellow that she felt she had known from another "time". His name was Duke Dudley. He was delightfully charming and brought forth laughter from her heart.

CHAPTER ELEVEN

The Story of Martha

"Every incarnation that we remember most increases our comprehension of ourselves as we truly are..."

Aleister Crowley

It was very unsettling to learn about a sister from a past life who was so resentful of me. I asked Richard if we could get more information. I thought it was fascinating that my present guide RX was called Matt in a previous lifetime that involved a sister that was unknown to me.

I couldn't possibly have recalled Eve in my subconscious if I never knew she existed, I maintained. Nor was Richard aware of these people previously. The amazing thing about his gift was that he could describe in such detail, not only how each entity looked as they came to him, but how the entity perceived us. For example he saw that to Matt, I still looked like Martha from the 1800's, young with long dark hair. So he obviously didn't see me physically but saw how my soul expressed to him. That was fascinating.

This made me think of how we see people in dreams. Their looks can be different yet we know it is them. This is something we must remember. The outer shell of a human being is but that, the outer covering, so has to be fleeting, and is not the real man. The real man, who still exists who is spiritual can touch bases with the higher self of the physical man. And this is what was happening with Richard. Rising above his five physical senses to his sixth sense, his higher self, was then open to connection.

I wanted to find out more about my past lifetime. I wanted to understand why I ran off with Matt, hurting my sister. One evening very soon after that Richard agreed to try and find out what had happened. After our prayer and meditation he drifted off into an altered state of consciousness.

* * *

The story began to come forth. Ricard became 'transferred' to that place in time in the early West. It was like he was actually there! He began to narrate:

> "I can see it! Matt, Martha and Eve and several wagons. Ten wagons, leaving from the East. Matt was the wagon master of the train. The plan was for Matt to marry Eve when they reached Oregon. He had already known her family, especially her father, who also came on the trip.
>
> "Now we're on the trip: The weather started out very good, but it was a long trip. Now, during this time Matt is getting to know Eve and Martha better. Even though they look a lot alike, both very pretty, their personalities are

very different. Eve is more outspoken and more self-centered. Martha is the quiet one, more giving, keeps things to herself.

"Yes, I can see the long dresses now, the blouses and long skirts. Surprised the women didn't wear pants...

"Eve complained a lot... about the food, conditions, and circumstances, while Martha was always positive. There is another man, named Josh. He's got his eyes on Martha. How interesting. He's a very tall slender man. He seems to pay more obvious attention to Martha. For some reason Matt seems to be bothered by it, even though he's starting out a new life with Eve. Matt knows this Josh. They are not friends, but just acquaintances. Different types of men.

"I can see them mixing. Eve seems to be bored with Matt and starts to go over and talk to this Josh. Being that Eve and Martha look so much alike, it was very easy to be attracted to both. And then, Matt walks over to Martha. They talk about the horses and trying to figure how they are going to get more food for the horses. Matt is discovering the qualities in Martha that he wishes that Eve had.

"As the days go by, even though there are not words between them, there is a growing rapport.

"Now we are getting out west, possibly is the Rockies. Very high. The weather is very cold. There is a problem with the horses and the elements. Looks like a real storm. Matt is trying to settle things down, but there is more work than people. The women are staying inside the wagons. There is a wheel stuck. They are trying to push these wheels out. Here comes Martha getting out in the elements, right along with the men, working... and they push. Their efforts finally succeed.

"At daybreak they proceed on their journey. Matt is totally in disbelief and surprised finding these beautiful qualities in Martha. He is falling out of love with nagging Eve and more in love with thankful Martha. Eve sees this, but her pride and ego will not let her talk about it. This Josh is satisfied to have either woman, so he'll dangle.

"Time has passed. There are three days left on the trip. The weather is nice. Beautiful night. In fact it looks like they are dancing to celebrate nearing the end of their journey. Matt dances with Eve... and then he dances with Martha. The chemistry is felt strongly. Martha takes a walk while the others are dancing and the music is going on. She is very emotional. She is finding herself in love with a man who was promised to her sister. She is fighting this. Matt looks for her and finds her sitting alone. She is not completely alone. She has her dog with her. She is petting the dog and talking to him. She has a kind way with animals and the only woman who was concerned about the animals on the trip. Matt approaches her. Her heart is all stirred up. She is having strong feelings for him, not knowing how he would respond. Then Matt tells her how his feelings have changed and that she is the type of woman he wants and has always been looking for. They hug and embrace. Then they kiss each other for the first time. Their emotions are very strong, there is something very beautiful there as he looks into her eyes.

"Matt says, 'I am going to leave Martha. Leave with me. Start a new life with me.' Martha hesitates for she does not know what to say or what to do.

"'I will wait for your answer. I am leaving in three days.'

"During the next couple of days, Eve senses something is happening. She becomes very withdrawn and bitter, not only to Matt but to everyone; yet, she keeps this Josh encouraged sensing that her world was about to change.

"The last two days were unbelievable. The rains came down heavily, constantly. Many were getting sick because of the cold and damp weather. Supplies were almost gone. There was an anxious hanging, knowing they were so close to the end of the trail; and yet it seemed to be so delayed because of the weather. I can see the rain hitting so hard on the wagon that it tore the canvas on it and the family on the wagon had nothing to cover themselves while the canvas ripped. They have a little baby with them that was already sick and not getting better. This wagon has to be abandoned now, and the family of four is divided into other wagons. There is no place to put their possessions. I can see the tears on the young woman's face as she has to throw out special things to her that had been kept in the family for a long time. There just is no room. Matt says he is sorry but the weather is so bad there is no time. The wagon is left behind. The weather is so bad you can't even see. The little boy from the abandoned wagon sees how upset his mother is and watches her throw away her very special vase. He decides to run after the vase, after the thing that seemed so important to her. It was dark. The mother was not aware that he left. As soon as she discovered he was gone she went into a panic. Her husband and the men quickly went out to look for him. Matt is torn because he has to tell everyone to keep moving because of sinking into the mud. Martha hears the mother screaming. She cannot go because she is holding the sick baby. Martha jumps out of the wagon and makes the wagons stop.

"'Wait! just for a bit!' she yells. She grabs her dog who was just standing there in the downpour and they ran out to look. But they never found the boy... the boy was lost... never to be found. Martha returns with tears streaming down her face knowing that the wagons have to go on... have to keep moving...

"Matt's love for Martha grows as he sees the courage of this woman. They are just about at the end of their trail. They will be there in the morning. Most everyone is asleep, but Martha is still awake. It looks like she is trying to feed the horses. It is very cold and wet outside.

"Matt comes up to her and says, 'I'm leaving. I can't live with Eve. I've told some of the others. There will be another to take over the wagons and bring them in. I cannot live with Eve knowing I love you. Will you go with me? Now?'

"Martha pauses. Her heart is torn in two. She thinks about the loyalty to her sister, then the love she has for Matt that is so great now. She can't give Matt an answer. She leaves to pray. The dog follows. As she prays she looks up to the sky. 'Please God. Help me. Tell me what to do.' She feels more torn than she ever had in her whole life, a horrible feeling. She knows Matt doesn't really expect her to come because he knows her sensitivity. He is getting the horse and wagon ready. Martha sees this. She thinks about how short life can be as her heart feels the painful loss of the little boy she was so fond of. No one can know the certainty of tomorrows. She walks over to where Eve still sleeps. She whispers to Eve. 'I'm sorry. I love you. Please try to forgive me...' Then she starts to walk toward Matt's wagon. It has started to move. She runs, her dog follows. She cries out, 'Matt, wait!' He turns around in disbelief. The woman of his dreams is running towards him.

"Matt and Martha were never to be seen again by Eve. She ends up with Josh. She uses Josh. Never loved him. Always wondered what it would have been like with Matt. She hates her sister.

"Matt and Martha pull into a town in Oregon and that is where they settled; Martha, Matt and the dog. But the dog has gone through so many hardships that once they get into town, the dog lies down. With a look of devotion on his face, he dies. He had given all he had because of the love he felt for Martha. Again she felt a great loss, for all her life she felt this dog was her greatest friend."

* * *

Richard had to stop. My whole being was reliving the story with him. I was overwhelmed. We talked about this new phenomena. I wanted so badly to share this with others. I knew I had to know more. He agreed to try another night.

* * *

Richard continued:

"After Matt and Martha had left the wagon train they never saw anyone connected with them again. Josh went to California to look for gold. He would be away for long periods of time prospecting. Eve didn't mind since she was not in love with him. She totally blamed Martha for taking Matt away and went on for years in a dream wondering how it would have been if it wasn't for what she had done. Deep in her heart she cared for Martha, but on the surface she was very resentful.

"Matt had money saved up. He decided to open a general store in town. It didn't take much in those days. Matt and Martha ran the store he bought. This was in 1874.

"Within a year Martha got pregnant. She was to have one child, a girl she named Sarah. Even though Martha was busy trying to help work in the store and raise Sarah she felt Eve's hatred and it started to drain on her. She got ill. She was devoted to her family and still had the same pioneer attitude she took when she went across the Oregon trail. Her health problems were brought on by her subconscious guilt of betraying her sister. Matt had a notion that was the root of her illness.

"Martha lived only ten more years with her little girl. Matt took Martha's death very hard. It was a strain and a reminder to raise little Sarah. He became withdrawn and detached from her.

"As Sarah got older, about fifteen, she fell in love with a young man who wanted to go to California. She felt that her father wouldn't really care, and might even be relieved in a sense. So Sarah went to California with the young man. She left in the night, leaving behind a note to Matt. When he found the note he was very saddened. As time went on he realized he had lost everything. He was never to see his daughter again.

"Matt ran the store alone. He was a good man and there were women attracted to him, but his heart belonged to Martha. He clung very hard and kept reliving the past. He died about five years later of depression."

* * *

A sudden thought came to me. I asked Richard if my daughter Sarah from that lifetime was the same daughter I had in this lifetime. I had remembered a dream I had sometime back. It was as if I had died, for I was looking down from above. I saw a graveyard all run over and a young girl kneeling by this grave. I came closer and realized that was my grave, and the girl was my daughter. I never forgot that dream.

Richard after a moment said, *"Yes. The same daughter then as now."*

Tears welled up inside me to think my daughter and I in that time were separated so young. No wonder I felt so drawn to be near her. Thank God I had a chance for another lifetime with her.

Richard went on, *"And the man she left with was the Dudley man. He became a gambler."*

The Dudley man was the man she was seeing now! He seemed to have similar ways: flamboyant, good looking, yet with a certain sadness within him. Something unresolved there.

* * *

Sometime after this information came through, a message came forth from my mother: *"Vikee. I am so excited about your breakthroughs and communications. My main project is a loving guide and help to Annette. I am with her more than she realizes. She will get stronger as the days pass.*

I cannot tell you how important your work is. Don't let anyone take you away from it. Love, Mother."

* * *

Richard had finished his story. I was very emotional as I pondered over everything. I knew this information came forth to help me understand myself and also Eve. Maybe by reliving this Eve could see that Matt would have left whether I had gone with him or not. Also in the long run, it is not fair to yourself or the other person to marry someone you don't love. My love for animals, especially dogs, followed me into this time, I always had one in my life ever since I could remember and a deep compassion and concern for animals. I remembered this inner feeling of gratitude I always felt for modern conveniences around me, thinking back many times how it must have been in the old days. Many times when I was driving on the highway the thought crossed my mind of how long it would have taken if I had been going by wagon train. I could see why I felt many anxieties in this life over weather conditions when travelling, especially over mountains. Then I remembered the deep sadness I always felt for lost little children, to the point of tears and dreams over it.

* * *

I have learned that each soul is working out their karmic debt or lesson that they created in the past or past lifetime. There is a reason for everything that happens to people. There again, the law of cause and effect. Perhaps the couple on the wagon train that lost their boy had neglected or abused a child in another lifetime. It is very important to learn, when we can, the causes of situations, and then forgive and detach from them.

If I had believed I was doing the right thing at that time or any time, even now in this life, I must have the faith to be honest and back up my belief. This would have faced the situation and dissolved the guilt. I died over that guilt in my last life.

Everyone has a choice as to how they react to every decision or disappointment that comes in their life. They can either grow through that experience or become more bitter and cling to it. I thought about Eve. I prayed she would be open to this soul searching and forgive, not only me and Matt, but herself.

If we could all look back into past lives, or at least go back as far as we can remember now and see how memories and emotions are carried over it would help us to understand why we feel the way we do. The importance of this is to take any bad memories or feelings and try to release them by totally feeling love and forgiveness for all. This is not always easy to do and this is why it is so important to work with these truths, to be able to live a happier life.

The thought came to me, because Matt and I did not honestly face our feelings with Eve and "ran out on her unaware", we lost the opportunity to be together in this lifetime.

I was grateful for Richard's "look into the past". There was much to think about.

CHAPTER TWELVE

Richard and Lynne

From the time Richard had returned after Jason's death, he had been very busy. There was a lot of upkeep around my house and grounds, and time spent every day for meditation and prayer. His previous employer from the health food store was happy to have him back.

Richard had not made any attempt to find out about Lynne. He felt it was better to leave well enough alone. Because she was connected with his music world, he also put that aside for the time being.

One day while he was working at the store he looked up. The customer coming into the store was Lynne. She had heard that he was back but said she didn't contact him as she was in the middle of her marriage breaking up. Her husband was very jealous and followed her a lot she said. But, she added, things had tapered off and she was beginning to feel more relaxed as her divorce neared it's finality.

Richard was very happy to see her and to hear she was now free, so they began to see each other again. From the time she walked in the store, she needed his help in one way or another. He began to have less time at home.

* * *

One evening when we were receiving messages, the following came through: *"Richard, your chances of a good future with Lynne will increase if you continue on in your work for now and be patient. She needs this time to develop her own strength. Send positive energy and love to her. Love, Queen Gianna."* Queen Gianna had come to us many times as an adviser and had revealed she had been in a lifetime with Richard, centuries ago.

Another time my mother brought him a message: *"We are helping you so keep praying for you and Lynne. She could be right for you but not now. It would be hard to live with her now. You must remember what you are really there for."*

Another message from K.W.; *"Richard is going through a karmic period. He will have many tests before he reaches the next plateau."*

The messages were given much thought. Now that he had found Lynne again he was hoping she would be open to his spiritual life. He explained what had happened in his life and he was hoping she would be open. Lynne was fascinated. She started coming to the house a lot when Richard channeled.

Prior to this I had met some spiritually enlightened people both at the classes I attended, and the ones I had given. One special teacher named Joan and I had a special rapport. Once one really wants to grow and learn, it was like a door opening and a new world of adventure pouring forth.

I invited Joan to my house to give a class. She had not met Richard previously. She came with another lady named Anna, a psychic with very wise eyes. When she and Joan met Richard they looked at each other knowingly. They "knew" he was a chosen one. They said they had all been together in Jesus' time. He was informed he would be going through body changes and preparations in order to be able to receive more easily messages from higher dimensions.

Richard was at a crossroad. He was very devoted to his spiritual studies, but he was also very human. Lynne in the meantime was pressing him to move in with her. She tried to convince him how much she could help and assured him that he would have all the time he needed for his meditation and spiritual work. At first he hesitated, because of the messages cautioning him, but he felt if Lynne was that supportive, it could all work out, even if she did have two young girls.

That night, with Lynne present, a message came through for her: *"You must realize fully who you are with. Richard belongs to his work for All. It is a gift for you to be with him. If you are to be his love, chosen one, you must not question his love or sincerity. He needs to spend much time in preparation. He will need your support. Decide soon your path, for he is in His praise. We love you. Your blessed friends."*

Lynne assured Richard everything would work out. He had been alone so much of his life and felt such a strong love for her, he moved in with her.

* * *

At first it was like a dream come true, living together as a family. Lynne was a very good cook, an immaculate housekeeper, and affectionate to extremes. Richard surely thought he was in heaven. They moved to a larger apartment out of town as Lynne wanted to be away from everyone. He quit his job thinking he would get one closer to where he was living. But it didn't work out that way.

As the weeks rolled into months, the accumulation of certain happenings led Richard to see things in a different light. He was very fond of Lynne's girls, helped them with homework, and had little talks with them, but it bothered him to see how jealous Lynne was of his time with the girls, or anyone but her. Quiet time was at a minimum with his new family life. He wasn't used to the chatter of ten and thirteen year olds, especially when their friends were around the loud music took over. Though he spent many hours looking for work, he seemed to be blocked in getting a job.

Anna had said that he wouldn't be getting work in that town away from the dedication of his studies. I hoped for his sake she was wrong. Everytime my son came over to help me, or to channel, Lynne either tried to block or delay his coming. I felt apprehension with her obsessive clinging. I was hoping it would work out for Richard's sake and he could help her get over her deep insecurity. He called me less and less as the months went by.

* * *

I began to compile all the messages and information that had come forth. I felt they had to be shared; my book was to begin.

CHAPTER THIRTEEN

Keeping in Touch With Jason

"Those on the 'other side' want to communicate with us for several reasons. They are anxious to let us know that death is not the end."

"The Dead Are Alive"
by Harold Sherman

On behalf of the multitude of people suffering from grief, I am inserting additional messages from Jason after his death. By sending out prayers and being receptive to communication, it can be revealed that life does go on and the departed are not far away. This knowingness will change the attitude of grief, thus helping both the loved one that has left, as well as the one left behind.

I kept a separate record of my messages about or from Jason, from the time of his passing. At that time he had been painwracked and resentful. Those of you who have lost a mate through death can understand why it would mean so much to know how he was, and to be assured he was still existing.

Richard hadn't begun getting direct contacts until Jason had been gone six months, but I had been trying to communicate through automatic writing.

Because I was too emotional at times, I usually did much better when Della and I were together keeping our thoughts more balanced. Since she lived in the Bay Area, I didn't see her as much as I would have liked.

* * *

The following are some of my messages that have not been previously shared:

October 1984, one month after his passing. From my guide, RX: *"Jason is sleeping most of the time. Your loving thoughts pull at him in a loving way. He can feel what is coming from your heart. He is trying... Keep praying for him. In between sleeping he is trying to progress because he realizes now how much you loved him and were trying sincerely to help him. The more you send peace and be less emotional, the more it will help him. Your mother and others are also helping him. He is releasing his hostilities as you keep sending as much love and light as you have been. Keep your faith. Encourage him to awaken to his new learning world. Live your life."*

* * *

When an entity wants to give a contact or message it is much easier for them to come through direct if your mind is open and clear. When they try to come through another person such as a medium or channeler it is much harder. This takes more energy force and it is hard to maintain that energy for very long. This is especially true for those newer to the spirit world. It is important to realize the importance of raising the state of consciousness to a higher vibration, by meditation or prayer.

* * *

Three months later Jason's passing came the following message through pen: *"Hi my dear. I sleep a lot but feel better. I am grateful for your prayers, but I wish you would release me more. That is the best way you can show me your love, not to grieve. It is not necessary. I am here. I must thank all these souls who helped me give you this message. Tell my little Nikki I am watching over her. Love always, 'Papa' Jason."*

* * *

Between Christmas and New Years: *"You know I am with you in spirit during these holidays. This will be the first without you but at least your kids will be there. I will be with you when you see the new year in. Do not be sad. Love is never apart."*

"It will be easier after the holidays, Jason, even though I know you are near.!" I added, "Where were you Thanksgiving?"

"Sleeping. Release and know I am watching over you."

* * *

January 1985: *"Hi Vik. Now that the holidays are over you must get rid of things. I am trying to help you. You need the money. Sell one of the cars and get the boat ready to sell, and all my things. You are starting a new life now, Vik. I love you!"*

* * *

Message from Jason through Richard, six months from passing:

"Vik. I can see... feel... what is going on. I am proud of your attitude. I like seeing you busy and more involved in life. Give my Nikki a kiss from her papa." I assured him I would. She dreamed of him often. She spoke of him as naturally as if he was in New York, instead of beyond.

Not long before Jason passed away he said, "When I get on the other side, I will have to let you know I'm still around." Then he thought about lights. "If I can, I will flicker lights to let you know I am keeping an eye on you," he mused. I had forgotten that conversation until Annette mentioned one evening how the lamp in the bedroom was flickering. The ironic thing was, a song was playing on the stereo that was a favorite of Jason's and mine. I ran in, delighted, and Annette and I danced around to the music. It was called "Raindrops". I remembered to ask Jason the next time Richard channeled, about the lights.

"Yes Vik. It is us reminding you that we are around and helping. Don't ever worry about being alone, ha ha... Jason."

* * *

The following messages were scattered through the next year: *"Hi Vik. Don't worry about your car. You know how I feel about them. It will all work out. Just stay open and it will work out spontaneously. Wait and see."* (and it did, I "fell into" a good deal for another car). *"I wish I could tell my mother that I am doing well. Someday I pray she will understand. I would like to get through to her. I feel like I owe so much to her as I was a rebellious type of child. Perhaps someday, the opportunity will present itself. Remember that I always will love you and will help you when I can. But now, I have to concentrate on me. I know you understand. I am a lot happier now, thanks to you... and your prayers... and love. Goodbye for now. Love always, Jason."*

* * *

The following months: *"Hi my love. I understand you far more than I ever could have, being there. It is true when they say you cannot see the forest for the trees. Well, that was me. But now I feel that we are both doing what you always wanted us to do. And that is to work together on higher principles. You would be proud of me. I'm making things up to you, making it up to others... Love, Jason."*

* * *

Dozens of messages came through, but many would be trivial to anyone but myself, so I will end this section with the following message I received the spring of the following year.

"Hi Vik. *I see spring has begun. So has your path opened more clearly, so begin. Tell sis to be open and that I love her and mom. They will understand in time. You have our loving help and guidance with you. Acknowledge it. Be open to it when you need it. All your messages are with much love. You do not need me for your work. I must go on to other work. I will be with you when you call me. We both have a lot to do Vik, me from here, you from there. Your life will be good and rewarding. Love can never be separated. I know that now. Carry on, my love, Jason."*

* * *

In sharing these meaningful messages, I hope to show how much one can progress, even though physically separated from loved ones, how much prayer can help them as well as ourselves. Grief holds everyone back.

If your precious departed spoke to you right now, they would ask you not to hold them back by your emotions, but to release. Know they are but a thought away.

You can communicate if you have the faith in your ability to do so. If you believe that God is eternal life, then also realize that man as His counterpart will also continue to express life, no matter how far away it seems to be. As you become more open to this and sit quietly in meditation, you will become attuned to a higher vibration, reaching past the five senses. There you will rise above the emotions and turmoil of earth, and feel at one with all. Remember this when tears start to come. Send out that oneness of love and light, not sorrow and regrets, across the "bridge... to the other side."

CHAPTER FOURTEEN

Richard Returns

It had been over six months since Richard had moved in with Lynne. He had never felt so many emotional ups and downs in his life. Because of his feelings for her he tried to overlook her jealousy. The situation did not improve. He felt bad because he had not spent nearly enough time in meditation or even talking to his spiritual friends, Joan, Anna, myself, and others.

Lynne's girls kept playing loud music, but she did not want Richard to correct the girls in any way. He loved the girls and tried to overlook the drawbacks of the noisy atmosphere as he had always wanted to be part of a family, travelling so much. He could get away only on rare occasions without Lynne getting upset. He found it wasn't worth confronting her with his needs for solitude. She did not understand. It was strange. He seemed able to pick up only temporary work. Permanent jobs were strangely unavailable.

Though I saw Richard very little, one evening he came to a group meeting. Everyone was so happy to see him. Joan, Anna and another girl named Tammy, among a few others were there. Tammy was around Richard's age, and had studied the Mariel method of healing. Richard knew her from before as he was deeply interested in doing healing work; and had helped many people. Back near this radiant girl again, he began to realize how much of his true work he had let go.

During our meeting a knock came at the door. It was Lynne. When she saw Tammy there, she became very upset. She whirled around and went back out the door. Richard tried to get her to come back in, but she wouldn't and left. She called a short time later, demanding he come right home. Through his embarrassment he stood his ground. He began to see things as they really were. He told her he was staying back in the cottage and would drive out and talk with her in the morning when she had time to cool down.

The next morning when Richard came in from the cottage he told me he was going to tell Lynne he needed more time there for his spiritual studies. His meditation through the night brought great peace to him again.

Upon arriving at the apartment he was shocked to see that Lynne had cut off her dark long hair, knowing how much he loved it long. He told her he needed to get away for awhile to get back into his true work and quietness. She became hysterical as he packed and tried to keep him from leaving.

Richard was shaken as he drove away. He realized he could do nothing at this point but pray for her, for she would not listen to reason. He was heartsick, feeling a failure, still loving her. But loving her was not enough; he had to leave.

* * *

In my concern for Richard over these last months I had talked of Lynne to Anna and Joan wondering why she was so possessive of Richard. They both knew why. They said his last life time was two thousand years ago, in Jesus's time. He had not returned since. He chose to come back at this time to help others, but found himself out of step with the fast pace of this age. Lynne was his wife in that lifetime. This explained why he was so vulnerable and drawn to her. She was possessive of him then because of his desire to walk the spiritual path with Jesus and follow his teachings and journeys. Lynne has lived other lifetimes since that time, but unfortunately did not get over her deep sense of insecurity and jealousy in her relations with others, thus she kept those emotions with her.

The interesting thing is she had another opportunity to overcome this through her love of Richard and his dedicated loyalty to her. He tried to help her understand, but she was overpowered by negative emotions. He knew he had to go on...

PART II
"THE CONTACTS"

CHAPTER FIFTEEN

The Messages Continue

Over the next few weeks As Richard was able to meditate more, messages started pouring in again. The following one was for me:

"Well, good to be able to reach you again. I am seeing progress in your soul, more light coming from you. We are excited about your book and efforts, Vikee. You are talked about, especially by your relatives and friends. But you still need harder work and dedication if you really want to help bridge the two worlds. I am fine and busy like most adjusted souls. But pray for those who are here and not adjusted. For it is a dark place in which they reside until they desire to progress. Remember, **prayers are like sunshine coming from a cloud**. King William."

* * *

A message came to Richard from a beautiful dark lady who said she had been a wife of his centuries ago in Ethiopia:

"Richard. I am sorry that things haven't worked out with Lynne. We tried to work with her too, for your sake. But you do not have time to spend trying to pull her along. I know you enjoy companionship, but there are not many like us on your earth anymore. So you must strengthen yourself... and everything will fall into place. When you need companionship at times, focus on us who love you. There is no time now for you to stay emotional. You are being helped and appreciated for your work to help bridge the worlds. I am proud of your healing work. Keep your faith. Love Always, Nora."

* * *

My guide speaks: *"**The truth is, that there are so many of us that want to communicate with you to assure you there is no real death, but only a continuation of the cycle. Communication will start becoming easier, for people are opening up more. RX.**"*

* * *

From Richard's master guide: *"Dear ones. You are getting to the stage where you should only try to get direct contact. Do not use the board or encourage anyone else with that method. Negative forces will do anything to turn you back and your emotions are your weak point. Do not let anyone dissuade you from us. Put self aside, for the higher. Remember your dreams. They can help you. We are always around. So pray for your world and all worlds. Do not give up. 'Z'"*

* * *

Another guide of Richards: *"You must learn patience. Things will get clearer for Lynne later. Do not listen to the world for only a few know the real way. You must go by your own pushings, for that is us pushing you. You will have all you want and need... if you will learn more patience. There will always be obstacles and delays on earth. It is meant to be that way. The most important thing is spiritual growth. Queen Gianna."*

* * *

From my mother: *"We are helping all of you. You must be strong. Don't take any frustration inside. Circle all in the divine light. All things will work out sooner with more positive thoughts and faith. Love, Patricia."*

* * *

From RX: *"It is so difficult to live on earth in harmony. It is important to try to awaken while you have a body. Then you can help others. Empty your mind so it may flow like a river. Do not judge, condemn, worry or intellectualize, attach or accumulate. Just live simply and keep your mind on the divine with everything you do. The more you act like a God, the more you will become one. Your friend and guide, RX."*

* * *

From King William: *"Vikee. Keep on studying and meditate especially now. We want to help and will give you more facts when you can tune in more effectively without emotion. Study your cards and dreams and start doing readings again. This will strengthen you. We will help. Sincerely, K.W."*

* * *

"My Dear Richard: We see that you are at a crossroad in your life. Detach or go alone is our request, for you must do our work.

We are watching. Solidify your spiritual nature. There are many that are looking up to you for this. Don't let them down. Above all, yourself. If you can't do it, then who can? My love always, Nora."

* * *

Richard received so much help from above, it made the transition easier away from Lynne. He did see her, but felt that until she really wanted to progress and rise above her entrapments, it would be better if they did live apart. Even though he still loved her, he knew she needed to find her own inner strength and not depend on others, as so many do, for their happiness. When we cannot help those we love, even when we are around them, then our releasing them in prayer to divine guidance is the best we can do for them.

* * *

From K.W.; *"You must remind yourself that you are in the most important stage of your life. Your mind must be clear and free of emotion so you will be able to dictate this great information. This is a critical time for your growth. It is best for you to be single at this time. Learn as much as you can, and pray for the world."*

* * *

On my father's birthday I sent him my thoughts of love. I received back the following message later, through Richard: *"My dear Donna. Thank you for thinking of me today. It is easy to forget these things when you are out of the body. Time is so entirely different here. Remember that... love never changes. True love that is. I have learned much more about love since my departure.* **It is not important what you are while on earth, but how you radiate your light and love to others. Let people appreciate and accept you as you are and not what they want you to** *be. I used to let others influence me... and have since learned. Don't worry about anything, we are watching over you. Love, Dad."*

* * *

My mother's sister, Cena, became gravely ill. I had been getting messages about her from my mother. When Aunt Cena was at the hospital we took her a message on tape to her from my mother. She listened with much emotion.

* * *

"My dear sister. Please do not fear. Everything will go very well, very smoothly for you. Just think of us and all of your loved ones over here waiting to see you. You will see so many that love you. You will be so glad to get out of that pain. Believe me, Cena, I know. Think of us constantly now. But most of all, think about God and pray. He will help you smooth your way, my dear. It's not that bad. Its normal to be a little afraid as the body seems to want to hold on. But just relax and release now. Let God take over... you will see how much happier you will be, I promise. Don't worry anymore about your children or any of the family. You can never be separated from them or they from you. You have had a good life, Cena dear, and a much longer one than mine was. We all love you and are with you. Relax and trust, dear. Your sister, Pat."

* * *

Cena grasped Richard's hand tightly as she heard the message that came from her departed sister. Richard then told her to reach out and contact him after she passed over. She gave a faint smile and promised she would try. She was seventy-six years old. Even though her body was in pain from her condition, she slipped over the next day in a peaceful sleep.

I wish to note that two months later she did *"come"* to Richard. She felt our prayers and was drawn to find us from our light. She briefly told us how grateful she was for our prayers and that she was resting. More contacts came later.

* * *

For Martha/Vikee about Eve: *"Eve is progressing. Your prayers and work have helped your sister. You have lifted yourself from old karma now. Many others could do this if they were informed and sincere. This is your job now. RX/Matt"*.

* * *

One evening my dear friend Lorna that had passed over several months previous came through: *"It means a lot to be able to reach over to you Vikee. Please tell my daughter that I am doing fine and am watching over her. Thank you for your prayers. Your friend, Lorna"*.

* * *

From my step-father: *"Just came by to let you know your thoughts are much appreciated."* (It was his birthday and I had sent him a prayer and love). *"You have to do things the way you see it, and not what others think. Goodbye, RMS (Sandy)."* We were happy at his progress.

* * *

Queen Gianna comes through: *"It is important to use the good power you have and focus more on what you really want in life. Concentrate. Draw it to you. Spend moments every day doing this. You will be amazed. Do not be selfish however. You must think of God. I was a queen and knew about power. Good luck. Queen Gianna."*

* * *

Regarding relationships: *"It does not matter what your status is, most of you are tied to another due to karma. So it is important to always live for God and not to impress others. Do the best you can, you cannot do another's work. Release your attachments. They must work out their own karma. Remember these words. King William."*

* * *

Another time K.W. said: *"My dear ones, please get this message also to Della. I have been observing your situation and I know how lucky you are. You have much help around you, so much support over here for your efforts. Have your meetings, unite.*

When you ask in a selfless manner you will always receive it. As time goes on more will be drawn to you, as people are drawn to sunlight. I am used to living in royalty. **You must learn to feel as a king inwardly, but walk as a humble servant outwardly. Be like iron on the inside and let no one, no negative thing penetrate.** *For the time is short and your work is too important. You will not receive frequent contacts from me shortly, for I am preparing for my next phase in a return to earth. Take my advice and continue to work hard. Do not underestimate your efforts and work. Best wishes and deepest sincerity, K.W."*

* * *

K.W.'s last message to us: *"All things will work out, the more positive thoughts are. There are many of you in your spiritual quest and will seek faster results unless distracted. Remember, as long as there is desire, there will be disappointment. You must find your own way, as others must find theirs. Live as we live, by letting go. Give yourself and your loved ones freedom. God's love is the greatest of all. Goodbye, K.W."*

* * *

The following messages came from RX/Matt: *"It is difficult to live on earth. It is important to awaken while you still have a body. Then you can truly help others. Empty your mind so it may flow like a river. Do not judge, condemn, worry or accumulate. Live simply and keep your mind on the Divine."*

* * *

"You must keep forging ahead. You will know what to do at the right time. Always strive for the Truth. Once learned and practiced you will be free from all karma."

* * *

"We are helping you, don't forget. The more you keep your thoughts high, the happier your soul will be. You must reach more people and express peace and joy. That is the way... joy. Live each day as an important day for the Lord. Do not waste precious time. You are all so loved."

* * *

One evening Richard was channeling for a group. The following came through from Matt:

"I would like to speak in behalf of us on this side. I am Vikee's guide, RX. My name was Matt in a previous lifetime. I was her husband then and her name was Martha. I am not what you call a really highly evolved soul. I guess I am like a blue collar worker. But let me offer some insight:

"Prayers are so needed and appreciated on all dimensions, for even on the lower realms where it is dark, a pure prayer is like a flashlight in a tunnel. And even if the entity is not completely ready to accept it, at least he sees the light. I am not a real religious man, but I have seen the power of prayer on this side. But the actual working out of karma is done with the body on the earth plane, making your time there very important. When you get here, sometimes you will see relatives and others, and sometimes not. Many create a world of their own from their desire nature which of course is not solid, but illusionary. Just as I am still comfortable with my last life with Martha. We all can learn more and hope to benefit each other more through the contacts. Thank you for your attention. Am wishing all of you well."

"Martha, Eve is doing better, thanks to you and your prayers for her. She is learning more to forgive, and is now anxious to go on..."

CHAPTER SIXTEEN

Communication From Famous People

"Death is nothing at all. I have only slipped away into the next room. I am I and you are you... Life means all that it ever meant. It is the same that it ever was. There is absolutely unbroken continuity..."

From Harry Scott Holland 1847-1918
Cannon of St. Paul's Cathedral

My son and I continued to work together and prayed for the continued unfoldment of this wonderful communication we were receiving. During his altered state, whatever came through, I either wrote down in speed writing, or taped, usually both.

* * *

It was nearing Thanksgiving time when I saw Robert Wagner being interviewed on television. I had adored him and his wife Natalie Wood. In this tender and nostalgic interview, he revealed his deep love for the wife he had lost. My heart went out to him in his pain of losing Natalie through such a tragic accident. I sent him prayers, and also to her, who had been gone two years now. Annette and I always felt close to Natalie through the years. She had been a special favorite of ours. When she drowned, we grieved along with her public.

That evening we received a shock. NATALIE WOOD appeared to Richard! She seemed disturbed over the fact that her husband was still so distressed and unhappy. She wanted to reach him. She spoke through Richard:

"Dear ones: I wish you would do me a service. I am asking you this because you loved me when I was there. You are also not well known people. It is important that you try. Bob is still distressed about me. Granted, my death was a tragic one, but it was my time, due to karma. A chance to make things better next time. He must know that it isn't his fault. He should not grieve anymore. It truly hurts me. He is a beautiful man and I love him dearly. Let him know I am okay and that he will see me and be with me again. Thank you for your support all of these years. Sincerely, Natalie Wood."

* * *

As thrilled as we were to receive this message from Natalie we were wondering how on earth we could reach Robert Wagner. And even if we did, why would he believe us? Through the course of the messages that followed from her, we tried in vain to reach him, through his studio and agent, but were never able to make the contact.

Some weeks later a second message came:

"Dear ones. I want you to try to contact my RJ again. Please try. He must know that I am okay and that I love him and am doing the best that I can. I have been sleeping a lot. I am not sure how to get a hold of him, but do the best you can. Once I *feel I have made contact then I will feel more at peace and free to go on. I wish my relatives could be contacted but I am afraid they are not open to this. I must go now. Try to help. Sincerely, Natalie Wood."*

Robert was just starting the series "Lime Street", so I wrote again to the studio. Not long after that, his little star Samatha died, and again, he was devastated.

The next time Natalie came I asked her to see if she could find Samatha, the little girl who just got killed that was working with him.

"What do you want me to find out? Bob is upset. His attitude is down. Please keep trying to reach him. I'll do what I can to locate this girl. I may not be able to. Please keep trying. Sincerely, Mrs. Robert Wagner."

* * *

About a week later we received another surprise from a recent famous passover:

ROCK HUDSON: *"Natalie told me about you. I am disappointed the way people are feeling about me. I would appreciate if you would pray to the world to release their emotion of me. For as painful as it was, I was able to destroy a lot of karma in this life. Few know me as I really am. I will rest and evaluate. Help others to release me so I may truly rest and get on with my evolution. Sincerely, Rock Hudson."*

* * *

It is important to note here that both famous people referred to "karma", the law of cause and effect. It is realized when passing over that each soul has different lessons to learn and they evaluate after passing over how each one was handled. That is why the continuous cycle of life is necessary, for growth of the soul in every experience brought to them, or that they brought to themselves.

* * *

Again we heard from Natalie:
"Dear ones. I am not giving up. I am trying to reach my RJ. He has dreamed of me more often now."
I asked, "Did he get any letters I sent him?"
She answered, *"No, unfortunately."* I was disappointed.
"What shall we do?" I asked her.
"Wait... I will try to make a circumstance more favorable in another way. Thank you again, Sincerely, Natalie Wood."

* * *

The next time Natalie came to Richard we asked her if there was something between her and Bob privately that he would understand and believe that she was really coming through.
"Ask Bob about the third ring... he will understand." Natalie.

* * *

By December she told us: *"Thank you for your help. Don't worry about the results. If your efforts do not bear fruit then I will try and contact another. My deepest regards, goodbye, Natalie Wood."*

* * *

We felt saddened we were not able to carry through her request. The next time Richard felt her presence we suggested she speak directly as if in a letter to her husband, which she did:

*"To the Man I Love. My sincere hope and wish is that you will believe in me and trust me. Please keep your mind and heart open. You must know that my love for you is as alive as ever. I am only a thought... a vibration from you... always. We will be

together again. Please believe. Release your emotion of me, but don't shut me out. Do not have any remorse. These people want nothing of you. They only wish to help me. I will always love you... always, Your wife."

* * *

To my knowledge Robert Wagner has never received any of these messages.

* * *

ROCK HUDSON returns: *"I still am troubled by the vibes of the masses. Try to send me prayers like you did before. However, my death opened up new light in research for the world, a karmic condition which was preordained for me. I still have to release public opinion, but when you are an actor it is so very hard to do. There is much sacrifice involved for public appeal. The greatest of all, is personal privacy. I would say that is the most sought after desire for celebrities. I will rest better as time goes by. Thank you for being open, Rock Hudson."*

* * *

The following month I was asked to give some classes in Stockton. My subjects were helping those who have lost a loved one in death; understanding that life is a continuing cycle; and the Power of prayer; and Communication.

* * *

Upon request, Richard channeled and counselled also.

* * *

The night before starting my series of classes we received an inspirational message from Rock Hudson again:

"You can tell your class, this is one of the few truths in life. The importance of understanding death to the fullest and making the transition a smooth one, it's all like a dream. Just like my life was. And when you look at your life you will see it just as I have seen mine. You must always be humble in spite of others building you up and not be attached to yourself or others. If I had it to do over again I would have learned more about spiritual teachings, but, karma outweighs the choice sometimes. I have learned that love and hate are almost inseparable on earth. My emotions brought me very little happiness. So teach your class that no matter how famous or popular one may become, its meaningless in comparison to true knowledge. This sounds like a letter. Thank you again. Rock Hudson."

* * *

One evening we had another surprise, a visit from RICHARD BURTON: *"Tell Liz, thank you for all the memories, fun times and added spice into one's life. Liz is the most beautiful woman, even when she gets mad. She did get mad at me once in awhile. I was not easy to live with. Never had been. Didn't like myself. But loved her. She had the impossible task of loving someone that didn't love himself. Tell her I think of her, and send her love. I am doing fine. 'A toast to a life of memories with Liz'... Richard (Dick) Burton."*

* * *

A week later: *"Elizabeth dreamed about me the other day. It seems to be painful for her to think about me. I wish that she would pray for me. I do feel bad that I wasn't better to her... and myself. This is what excessive drinking does. Remember that when you are involved with someone like me. Have compassion. It's not easy, I know. I wish I could contact her. Could you reach her to tell her to pray for me? You remember the great movie of* Cleopatra? *She was so great because she was acting* out what she really was in a former life! We were together then. Goodbye. Good luck, Richard Burton."

* * *

Another day Richard Burton returns: *"Good day my dear ones. Did you see my picture in the paper? (It was on the front page of the* Psychic Guide. *He was "seen" by many at a pub in Wales.) Been getting around a bit. I am spreading the news about you. Told you I would. I've always enjoyed the underdogs. Liz can help you. She helps the underdog. Anyway, we have a connection from another lifetime. I was your "scallywag" son, long ago. Can't stay long. Got to move around. Enjoying my freedom. Dick Burton."*

* * *

Not only was I shocked to hear about my connection with Richard Burton in a past lifetime, I was amazed at what was "seen" following the previous message.

My son could actually "tune in" to Richard Burton approaching a Catholic priest. Then he drank out of the communion cup and requested assistance to us in helping others understand the naturalness of communication between both dimensions. The priest apparently still caught up in his orthodox beliefs did not try to understand him or what we were trying to accomplish and they began arguing. Others gathered around and tried to help his plight, but the priest was closed to his aggressive manner and his request. Then the picture faded off.

After my son opened his eyes he looked sad and said, "There are many over there who still do not understand the importance of acknowledging communication. They are locked in their carry-over beliefs. We must pray for enlightenment on both sides."

* * *

Another time Richard Burton returned to be of help with added humor:

"I wish to help you. I will keep trying to let others know. You need proof for the disbelievers. I will tell you something just between Liz and I. Everyone knows of course I was her husband and a drinker, I may say, but how many knew I only wore boxer underwear! And she used to be mad when I didn't brush my teeth when drinking. She put up with a lot, but... If they only knew that the most beautiful woman in the world snored. I'm glad I did drink! Ha, ha, ha. All kidding aside, she would probably laugh if you told her these things. I heckled her a lot. It used to take her forever to put her face on, but a beautiful one it is... hey? Keep trying. I will try to help you. Tally ho. R.B."

* * *

Another favorite appeared much to our shock, from ELVIS PRESLEY:

"I am still very tired, and sleep most of the time, but I've heard of you and your true hearted effort to help. Enjoy your quiet, simple life, a life I never had. Even money could not really buy it. I always felt the weight of my fans. At first I liked it, but as the years went by it became harder to deal with, so I started taking drugs, drinking much more than I ever thought I would. It made me forget my responsibilities. Don't forget how lucky you are. Remember, with fame you will burn two flames. When I will return I will be no one special, Goodbye for now. THE KING... E.P."

* * *

Another time I questioned Richard about MARILYN MONROE. I had read that the star Madonna believed she was Marilyn reincarnated.

Richard replied, "She died of suicide due to drugs. Over-consumed with the misery of her life. Needs prayers. She is communicating with Madonna but has not reincarnated. She is trying to relive in her. Still frustrated there because of the frustration inside herself. Difficult when a suicide. Best she didn't return soon. Has lessons to learn."

* * *

RICHARD BURTON re-appeared. *"I am still trying to put a good word in for you. I come to Liz when she is dreaming. I try to reach her but she's got her mind on so many things, so busy. Actually, I wish she would slow down and have a drink with me. Have to go. Tally ho. Your, R.B."*

ERROL FLYNN was a favorite of ours from the past. I asked one night about him when my mother came through. Since she had always adored him, she said she would look into it. Some time later she returned with the following information:

"Hi Vikee. It's your mom again. I have been looking in regarding Errol Flynn as you asked. You know how I liked him too. He is not here. He has reincarnated. Be glad for him. All a part of the process. He is in Europe... Ireland. He will not be famous like he was before. Like many others, he chooses not to repeat the same active lifestyle, a life of no privacy which is a hindrance when the soul wants to grow. The people do not understand. **Everyone thinks they want to be a star. Only the wise know better. A real star is the soul that lets their light radiate...**"

* * *

CHAPTER SEVENTEEN

Other Famous People from the Past

"When I see nothing annihilated and not a drop of water wasted, I cannot suspect the annihilation of souls, or believe that He will suffer the daily waste of millions of minds ready made that now exist, and put Himself to the continual trouble of making new ones. Thus, finding myself to exist in the world, I believe I shall, in some shape or other, always exist; and, with all the inconvenience human life is liable to, I shall not object to a new edition of mind, hoping, however, that the errata of the last may be corrected."

Benjamin Franklin, American statesman and scientist
(1706-1790)

Through our excitement, the following souls came to Richard during the course of the many months to follow:

* * *

"Hello! (Richard describes a big smile on this mans face, and louder and deeper voice boomed out). Just thought I would come by. Can't get over what you have all done with my ideas. When I look over a city and see all that light, I am thankful that I was given the idea. It is wonderful to see what man can do, especially if he walks in harmony with all....telegram, by THOMAS EDISON."

* * *

Thomas Edison returns: "*Good day again! I just want you to know how supportive I am of your effort. It reminded me of what I had to do in my life to accomplish. If I had listened to the populace I would have never achieved my goals. For you see, other so called authorities don't really know. Real courage is taking this on yourself and knowing that you will get God's help... the spiritual help. The world is in turmoil and needs your efforts. Thank you for your persistence. I hope you all sincerely keep it up. TO QUIT AT ALL, IS TO QUIT TOO SOON. Sincerely, Thomas Edison.*"

* * *

(Note: I wish to insert the next message although he is not a known famous soul). My father's comments:

"Hi Donna. I am so proud that my daughter and grandson are respected by such a great soul as Mr. Edison. I am trying to help you with your bookwork. Very impressive research so far. We are all excited about your efforts and your classes, for you are making the effort to bring about what we all want, a clear bridge between the two dimensions. You must believe that you are being helped. We have seen some special things happen with you both as of late. It is stimulating and inspiring to all of us. Don't forget to use your dictionary. Your eternal accountant, Dad."

* * *

From the most famous psychic who broke the Houdini code and worked with Ruth Montgomery from the "other" side:
"Congratulations on coming over the bridge! You've done it! I found team work essential, so stay together as long as possible. I was hoping for more progress since my demise. We're watching, waiting, hoping that more of you will emerge and pick up where we left off. You know what I had to say was reality. I must say now, that here I can see it all, even clearer and not as much restriction. Go to the Edgar Cayce Foundation. You will find supporters there. It is time to go full board now, I am pulling for you. I KNOW THE KEY IS MAKING MORE CONNECTIONS ON BOTH SIDES. THE WORLD IS IN DEEP NEED OF THIS SIMPLE TRUTH. ARTHUR FORD."

* * *

From one of our greatest presidents: "We are disturbed with America. I wanted America to be free, but too many have abused their freedom. Our country should have a good economy and a good environment. I was startled for awhile when I first passed over, but am awake and watching now like so many of our devoted leaders. We are in a bind because there are so few good leaders available for our century. I am not a great religious man but I still ask you to pray for the right guidance and leadership. ABRAHAM LINCOLN."

* * *

Another time Abe returns:
"Dear Ones. It is my wish to thank you for your contact. Don't give up for there are a lot of believers, especially in the

south. I will be returning soon and will have important work after the turn of the century. I will be reborn soon and will take my desire to pickup where I left off before. Wish me well. Keep up the fighting spirit. HONESTY IS STILL THE BEST POLICY. Very Sincerely, Abraham Lincoln."

* * *

From one of our greatest scientists:
"My life was devoted to science and mathematics. I know now that my search was for understanding. When I left the world I realized that I was on the right track concerning matter and energy. Yes, it is true, matter is always changing and that is the energy that transforms matter. The yogi of India understood this long before I did. So in that vein, it is illusion. This can only be realized by your own spiritual transformation. SEND POSITIVE THOUGHT TO ALL MATTER AND YOU WILL FEED ITS VERY ESSENCE. THE KEY TO THE TRANSFORMATION OF TIME. ALBERT EINSTEIN."

* * *

We had read that Thomas Edison and Henry Ford had been friends. HENRY FORD speaks:
"I was told about you from my friend. I see they are still making my cars. I must say, however, I like the older models much better. You put more personal attention to each and every one because of the smaller amount manufactured. Also, must say, much of the spirit is gone. When I first made cars they were like a luxury, but still affordable and everyone appreciated them. Now I see everyone with an automobile and only a few seem to really care about their car."

I asked, "Does it make a difference to its performance how you feel about your car?"

"Of course it does!" he exclaimed. "The more you communicate with your car, the better it will communicate with you and will work better for you. We built automobiles to last a good twenty years. Now they last for five. Why? Because of the abuse and negative attitude of the people. I must ask you to appreciate your car. You will certainly pay if you ignore it, as with all walks of life. SUCCESS IS DRIVING IN THE MIDDLE LANE... August, 1909. Henry Ford."

(Note: We looked up that date at the library and it seems to be his most exciting time... when he brought forth his Model T.)

* * *

(This message came as the baseball season climaxed with the world series beginning).

"It is sad to see what has happened to the "game". In my day we had to work harder, travel harder, and nurse our own injuries with little medical help. But we had a responsibility to our fans and community. There were no such things as drugs, only a little booze with some players. It was good to have the kids look up to their heroes. Now, the press has destroyed the children's heroes. PRAY THAT THE GAMES WILL BE MORE LIKE IN MY DAY. THE COUNTRY NEEDS THAT. I could not save myself with my illness, but the love I felt from so many helped me so much when I left; therefore, I understand your courageous step to better life and death. Sincerely, LOU GEHRIG."

* * *

We received special greetings on October twelfth:

"Good tidings to you all! When I discovered your land it was barren and beautiful. It is nice that they made a day for me to be remembered.

I sent over three ships. I lost a few crew members at sea. Sickness and plagues were dominant then. There was very little remedy like there is now. And hardly anyone in your land. Only Indians, which were hard to find."

I asked if the history books were correct.

"Not entirely," he replied. "But that is history. Not everything is entirely correct. When things are documented it is not usually from the one who sees, only the one who writes about it."

I asked if there was anything he wanted to add regarding his journey.

"There was too big an issue made about the world being flat or round. There were many others who believed as I did even though I received the credit. We did learn more about time changes and that was not brought out."

I asked Columbus if he had reincarnated since that time. *"I have been back in a lifetime in the days of the West. I did return to America since I discovered it. I took on the life of an ordinary farmer in the Midwest. Nothing special but I needed a low key life after being in the limelight so long.*

Remember, the soul remembers, and you can choose how you want to express that nature on this side. (I also had light colored hair in those days). Signing off as you know me, on this day. SIR CHRISTOPHER COLUMBUS."

* * *

A Memorable Birthday

The highlight of my last birthday (though I like to be thought of as "ageless") came after dinner when only Richard and my daughter were still present. Richard was anxious to fall into trance as he knew there were many from the "other side" wanting to be heard. I was shocked and thrilled as he began, to hear many wonderful felicitations pour out from my family and friends.

What I wish to share are the following messages from my famous friends, recorded on tape:

"Happy birthday, my dear. A toast to a marvelous soul. You are becoming quite a star yourself up here, I must say."

Perplexed, I asked, "I don't understand. By what we're trying to do?"

"Yes", he answered. "Your courage, determination and effort. I drink to that! Salute... tally ho. Your son from another "time". RICHARD BURTON."

* * *

"Dear friend. Thank you for your concern over me and trying to help. You are loved by many. Keep up with your work and shine like a star. Don't let others discourage you. Keep working with us. Yours truly, NATALIE WOOD."

* * *

"Enjoying this gathering here. Paying our respects and appreciation for your help. Thank you for listening to my cries and being truly understanding. Someday I will repay I promise. Please keep praying and sending your light to all of us. Thank you again, ROCK HUDSON."

* * *

"I would like to pay my respects to a special soul. I appreciate your original efforts. Being and thinking as a creator and inventor. That is wonderful. Do not listen to the people around you, for if you listen to them you will get nowhere. This is important for you to realize and remember. Because you send out so much light to us, you will have a golden light to surround you in your passing.

Please don't ever give up. You must always go with your intuition. We will help and guide you when we can. Remember that my dear and think of your ancestors and the ones who have accomplished things before. The dream must be first, then the power of thought building a strong impression, then continuing to focus on that will again materialize it into reality. Thoughts are electrically charged particles and atoms, and they can be just as much living as of course yourself. Have a wonderful celebration. We are celebrating with you also. MR. THOMAS EDISON."

* * *

Although not a famous person, I wish to add my husband's message on this special night:

"Dearest. It is so nice that others would step aside for me to speak with you. There are still many lined up here. But their love here is so great they are letting me through. I am so moved by all of your support. I could just kick myself for not being more understanding and supportive before. Please keep up with your work. I promise I will clean up my act before the next time around. You can always count on me, from now on. Happy birthday, with all my love. Jason."

* * *

I will conclude my happy event with the following from Richard's master guide "Z":

"As you see from your contacts, a soul is the soul whether he was famous or not. It is of no importance on this side, only what he has accomplished spiritually. This is neglected in many lifetimes. There will usually be at least one lifetime in which one is known or famous. He is learning different types of attachments such as power, pride, egotism that must be constantly faced when you are popular. So you see, it is not necessarily easier to be well known. This is the great illusion that we have. One would be better off to eliminate these drives and be content to be like a drop in the ocean. Better to comprehend a little, than to be confused with a lot. Remember this, and listen to your guidance from within."

* * *

One night Richard is able to go back several thousand years. He sees a brilliant light...... then a huge ark. He saw a very old man. He is dressed in Biblical manner, with a cane.

He speaks: *"I am very concerned about the welfare of my animals on earth. There are so many suffering and in pain. The world has not become a better place for the animal kingdom. Many species are completely gone, due to abuse of mankind toward them.* ANIMALS ARE THE SYMBOL OF THE EVOLVING SPIRIT, AND GOD TRULY HAS A GREAT LOVE FOR THEM. EACH DAY SAY A PRAYER OF PROTECTION FOR THE ANIMAL WORLD AND YOU WILL NEVER BE HARMED BY THEM. *Only prayer can persevere now. Hear my cries and bless them all, as you love animals as much as I.*

I am the guardian of animals. I will not return to earth. I am in my place....... NOAH."

CHAPTER EIGHTEEN

From The Unknown

"As a man casting off worn-out garments taketh new ones, so the dweller in the body casting off worn out bodies entereth into others that are new."

From the Hindu Scripture, The Bhagavada Gita

* * *

In this chapter I shall include messages through Richard from certain entities on the astral plane that may be of interest. It also shows there are different levels or planes of consciousness the entities are emanating.

* * *

"I am a twin sister of Elizabeth. Her name now is still the same as it was when she was a queen long ago. We were twins then and she was chosen over me. I still resent her. Now in her present lifetime she has become a world famous actress. Her life has had much inner turmoil because of what she has done to me and others in the past. She used her power to seduce the king so that she would rule again, as she did in the days of ancient Egypt."

I tried to dissuade her from the resentment that she had been carrying.

"How can I not resent what is rightfully mine, which was taken away? Even though she has paid, she has not paid in full because she chooses not to be happy with any man. I am seeing the change of heart. She is trying to find a stronger spiritual ground, but has a way to go. She needs to admit her faults and imperfection and apologize to me."

I reminded her that Elizabeth does not remember her now, but she stayed firm in her attitude.

"I will only accept her forgiveness. Goodbye for now. Carolyn."

* * *

The following message came through on the eve of Halloween:

"This is the time of year that most people remember me, I am a witch of the past. You can call me Clare. There were very few black witches, or bad witches. This has always been overstressed. Our goal is to work with the laws of the universe in order to benefit others in need. The world has always scorned at us and some were killed out of misunderstanding and ignorance. People did not understand. But we continued on to help the few that were open to us, and still are. Someday you should attend one of our gatherings and see for yourself. Remember that all we are trying to do is God's work. Tomorrow say a prayer for us. A prayer of gratitude may just grant your wish. Goodbye, for now. Tomorrow... Clare the white witch."

Richard described Clare as dressed in white. There were others dressed the same around her, in long white gowns and holding candles.

* * *

A man appeared from Roman days. He was standing in the background as Richard encouraged him forward. He described him as late thirty's and husky looking.

"I am a soldier under Pontius Pilate. I was there. Do not blame our leader for the fate of the Holy One. The ignorance of the people determined his fate. Yes, we were afraid of his powers but we were only going to put him away for awhile, for he did nothing. We saw no blame in Him. He was like no other man I have ever seen. Something in him moved us beyond our thoughts, We all, even the soldiers, felt a loss unexplained during his death. I must go. Goodbye."

He left before Richard could ask his name.

* * *

The same man appeared a week later: "I have come to you one time before. I am a soldier under Pilate. I want to leave here and I need your light to find my way. **Prayer is light.** If you could take some time to help me, I would be deeply in debt and gratitude. Call me Markus. I hope to make the next contact from somewhere else."

* * *

Another time a knight appeared: "It is erroneous that you may believe we all completely remember all the details of all our past lives. We forget much. When we are out of the body the soul does indeed remember highlights of various lives, but not most details. The more advanced soul can know more if it chooses. Some choose to forget all their lives entirely when they have become one with their creator. All of our conceptions of the whole are based solely on our levels of growth. But no one can see it all. Seeing is being. A knight's job is protection. You both will be protected. Thank you. 'B'."

* * *

It is now evident that many souls keep themselves locked in their own state of despair through the trauma of the event preceding their death. Such was Amos:

"My name is Amos. I am a black slave from the south. I am still here because of my hate for the white folks. My wife was taken away... the children beaten daily. I worked in the fields with a broken hand which took a couple of years to heal. You must understand that there are many blacks who have reincarnated and still have these deep resentments, due to this time. When you are around blacks who have shied away or seem mean to a white, what goes around, comes around. The women were always abused. The children that were born with a white father were always killed. I am reaching out for you white folks, for you are different. I hope that you will pray to the Lord Jesus, as I did. Thank you. And pray for the Negroes. 'Swing low... sweet chariot... swing low... sweet chariot... coming for to carry me home.'"

* * *

Amos returns another time: *"Thank you for your prayers. It helps to loosen these chains. There are many here like me. Thank you again for your prayers. Amos."*

* * *

Richard was told there were lower realms he had not seen. These were the realms of misery brought on by the deeds and motives and remembrances of the souls themselves. Their own consciousness of their misdeeds entrapped them, until they have a desire to see the light.

One night Richard spoke: "I see the lower realms, rapists, murderers, people with negative emotions that have enslaved themselves... their suffering is great. It saddens me."

"I see a man dressed in the time of 1800's. It is JOHN WILKES BOOTH! The man who shot ABRAHAM LINCOLN. He is surrounded by his remorse. He wants to get out. He requests prayer even though he feels he doesn't deserve it."

"Am going down further... way, way down... layers of darkness. A hellish realm... I see a man... ADOLPH HITLER! He is staring into this darkness. He sees nothing but darkness... it is cold. Like Siberia. He is so engulfed in negativity and darkness it might take a century of prayers to pull him out. I deeply pity him. I can't get through... walls and walls. Am coming back up." Richard was cold and shaken. We did much praying that night.

* * *

CHAPTER NINETEEN

From The Higher Ones

Richard and I realized how vital it was to pray for all souls. Being able to "see" the misery of the ones who had chosen a negative course increased his desire to raise his consciousness even higher, so he could be an instrument to be able to help more souls.

Through more meditation his master guide, "Z" had much to unfold. The following messages are all from him, as he appeared in his long white hair and old robes:

"As you see, you have made many contacts from different levels and dimensions. The possibilities are endless when you have completely surrendered your life to this high cause. As you surrender your life to this, more answers will emerge, even from the depths of your own being and consciousness. You have seen the results, so don't let yourself get sidetracked. The world needs you. You can make it better for everyone and do, when you are in prayer and devotion. God is endless... thoughts are endless... the universe is endless... you are endless. With love, dear brother."

* * *

"Give your life to God... and then you can see the past, the present, and the future. But only an empty vessel can go in any direction for it will not resist the gust of wind. You can only be filled when you can completely be empty. As your love for mankind grows, so will all the universe..."

* * *

"My Dear Ones. You must continue to do our work. Do not let others throw you off. You will have your spiritual center one day. We are helping. Go forward, and keep in contact. PRAY, MEDITATE AND ALWAYS KEEP GOD IN MIND IN WHATEVER TASK YOU UNDERTAKE. RADIATE LIGHT AND LOVE TO ALL..."

* * *

"My dear ones. It is good to see things opening up there. The important thing is to realize the essence of spirituality, which is the elimination of separate ego, and emerging of self to all. The ultimate self is no self. Be careful and observant of others, for it is easy to use these spiritual gifts in a spiritual materialistic fashion. This is why it is so vitally important that you and others spend the needed time firmly rooted in spirituality.

"Remember, you are receiving different contacts from different souls at different levels. You must always be open and realize the essence of your messages. Just because one has passed over does not mean he can tell you a lot, or even help you. It can be like a friend giving you advice about which house to buy. The advice is advice, so always look at the the source. *If you know the source to be higher than yourself then you must deeply dissect the truth and try as much as possible to utilize it in your daily life. That is spirituality. There will be times when it is better to listen to no one; when things become confusing and distracted. It is a signal for you to contemplate within yourself."*

"I can tell you truths. For example, if I take a trip, no matter how well I describe the experience it will still never completely substitute your own experience; hence, the greatest satisfaction is discovering your own truths and manifesting them. In this manner all will benefit from your sincerity and sanity. Excess will always yield to balance. **Look for balance in self and others."**

* * *

Note: This message came after Richard and I had seen the television movie special, "Out on a Limb", by Shirley MacLaine, in which a channeler brought forth information instrumental in changing her attitudes and views on life, past lives, and life beyond.

* * *

"The spiritual life is not rewarded by men. Life is an illusion. Live in a simple manner. Remember, lack is only in the mind."

* * *

"This is the message we have for you now... that of love. Your job is to love all, with no judgment, but unconditional love... and the knowing you can follow that path. Remember, you will always be where you are supposed to be. Do not let doubts or any outer thing weigh you down. Be happy and peaceful first then you can live any lifestyle with anyone. HAPPINESS IS DETACHMENT..."

* * *

"My dear ones. You must remember that what you call love is not really love at all... but an illusion of your clinging and separateness. It clings not. It demand not. Real love, which you will understand more when you are out of the body and more devoid of physical desires, has nothing to do with others' physically. It is giving totally, in which the giving becomes the receiving, in itself."

"RULES FOR TRUE LOVE: 1. HAVE NO EXPECTATIONS FROM ANYONE. 2. DO NOT ATTACH YOURSELF TO ANYTHING PHYSICAL, FOR NOTHING PHYSICAL CAN STAY THE SAME. THEREFORE, YOUR SO-CALLED LOVE BECOMES THE PAIN OF TRYING TO MAINTAIN SOMETHING THAT WAY, BUT NOW IS NOT. 3. TRUE LOVE YOU WILL NOT SEE, BUT FEEL, EVEN BEYOND THE HEART'S REACH. 4. LOVE IS FREEDOM TO LET EVERYONE EXPRESS THEMSELVES IN THEIR OWN WAY. 5. THE KEY TO REALLY KNOWING LOVE IS TO KNOW AND MASTER YOURSELF."

* * *

"It is good when you help another in spiritual confusion. There are so many seeking, and most are limited to their brief concepts of reality. It is all much more vast than mental comprehension. God can't be rationalized. Yet man continues to do so. This is where the error lies, in the religious differences. TRUTH IS BEYOND ALL DIFFERENCES AND JUDGMENTS. YOU WILL GROW IN TRUTH AS YOU GROW SPIRITUALLY. *You will look back and see it all clearly, but only when you've gone beyond common thoughts."*

* * *

"Remember, the Truth is always near, but you have to look for it within. As you see, there are so many ways to express the whole. And each has its valid point as due the elements of na-

ture. Have compassion and understanding. Your calling is not so much to convert others, but with a universal openness you can help another fulfill their calling, as we are all parts equal to the whole and will always lead to the whole. Teach others that the most important thing is to devote your fruit to God and all will flow in it's natural course. **Never judge. Pray for others. That is more powerful than words can ever be, for love is beyond language, and God is beyond love...**"

* * *

"Emotions are like a ferris wheel. You go around and round and are afraid to get off. When you are free of emotion, you can stand back and see, and not let it affect you at all."

"There is more reality on the 'other side' than here, although it seems like the illusion. There is so much life, more than we can comprehend."

* * *

At one of our group meetings when Richard was asked to channel, "Z" brought forth a message for them:

"Greetings. It is nice to have you all here tonight. We are all very fortunate that we can make this contact. The vibrations of many are contributing to this so called phenomena. As time proceeds there will be more of you inclined to do this work. But you must remember the importance of doing your own work before work can be effectively done for another. This is what prayer, meditation, contemplation and gathering of spiritual forces is all about. A means to a completeness."

"You must be thankful for being incarnated during this time period. If you think it is difficult at times, may I suggest that you go to the library and review life styles just within the last few centuries on earth. You will see that the struggled for survival was generally much more intense than it is today. No matter how difficult it may seem, it still cannot compare to hardships that you have all gone through in your past. Please take advantage of *your birth. Learn and grow with your knowledge. Shape it into wisdom, and with this wisdom open yourself and be giving to others who are ready for it. But you must use your intuition and guard this wisdom, for as it is stated, 'do not cast pearls before swine'."*

"As I feel each one in the room, I feel the genuine uniqueness of each. There is no need to be clones. But there is a great need to transform your uniqueness so that you can contribute to what you are, a complete spiritual being."

"Please take advantage of this time. Balance your lives with the physical, mental and spiritual, for once the spiritual is firmly planted, then it is much easier to enjoy the other two."

"What is SPIRITUALITY? It is love. It is compassion. It is patience. It is strength. It is right action, right speech, use of right knowledge and the sacrifice of one's lower self or ego as you call it, to the higher. I do not mean to belittle any of you, but there is no mind here that can completely conceive the whole. It would be like asking an ant to be his kingdom. Or it would be like asking a pebble on the beach to try and comprehend. No matter what you may think, it is greater than that."

"Always listen to others. Do not reject your brother. Utilize what you can. Do not worry whether another is wrong or right because you must realize that your conception is limited also."

"There is no time to judge others. There is only time to love... to give... and to grow. 'Z'."

* * *

The following messages were signed by "From Your Friends From Above", other higher guides:

"It is time for you to move forward, Release all attachments. Live in a simple manner and do not depend on others for your peace. Do not dwell on what you lack. Be grateful for what you have. The more you surrender to the Higher, the fast your answers' will come. Have faith in the good."

* * *

"You will find life easier by simplifying it. You are all so rich in material possessions. Discard or give away what you do not need. Do not unnecessarily clutter your mind."

"When you cross over into this dimension, you will see an illusion of time; the limitlessness of space, and the formlessness of form. You will see the many mistakes that were made and how you were your own worst enemy for limiting what you call God. And when you cross over, whatever your conception is, this will be what you will experience. Be it narrow, or be it vast."

"One last word about Truth. It is something that never changes. It is not subject to phenomena. It is unchanging, unceasing, all encompassing. You will find your greatest joy in seeking this, for the Truth becomes like a key to open the door to immortality."

"Remember these words and that everything on your plane is changing, other than these Truths, which you seeking."

"LOVE EACH OTHER, HELP EACH OTHER, AND DO NOT EVER BE ENVIOUS OF EACH OTHER, FOR ONE'S GIFT IS ALL'S GIFT."

"Keep praying and be thankful. Project only positive light and you can get nothing else."

"We are watching. We send our support and wishes."

* * *

"Remember this, you will always have questions concerning the path. Some will be answered and some will not. But it is not meant for us to know all, before we become all. In time we will. Remember that all scriptures are subject to interpretation. All will interpret differently so you must not rely too much on words. Look to yourself for answers."

* * *

"It is important to remember, that the hardest thing in life results from worrying about others. Do not worry about loved ones. Faith is knowing that they will be in their right place at the right time. Don't let anyone make you feel guilty for not being like them. You must be yourself. Each soul has their own special gift. Every soul has something to contribute to the whole, no matter what. Continue to think positively at all times. Don't give up. Keep your faith strong. You will become a better instrument as time goes by. Be humble around others, and helpful. We will do the rest."

* * *

"Remember, there is more reality on the "other side", our world, than on your side. It is more illusion where you are. There is so much life, more than one can comprehend."

* * *

"Time is of importance on earth, but not here; therefore, when you are over here it is easier to see future trends. Remember why you are there, to learn, love and work on karma. This is why astrology was created. Remember that much of your life is already set, due to karmic conditions. The more evolved you become, the more free choice you have. The ideal life is one of balance. Work and perform your duties. Grow spiritually, but learn. Make good use of your time. Love others, but do not judge. Trust your own intuition."

* * *

Friends From Above continue: *"There are so many of us who want to speak our mind. This is why we encourage you to develop so that you can tune in to all planes and beings. We all will help you as long as you are sincere in helping all. You see that both sides need communication so that we all can progress. Help us to contact more people so that the world can be saved."*

* * *

"THE MOST IMPORTANT LESSON IN LIFE is to have a positive outlook always. Faith and positive thoughts bring real happiness. Love others and serve others, but you must walk your path. Each must do his own work.

"DON'T WORRY ABOUT ANYTHING. If only you knew how much is already planned for you, you would see that to worry is indeed a waste. Be open, so you can let your path unfold unto itself. Remember, the more you can accomplish the sooner you will be in tune with God. We are all one, so have patience and compassion for all. But do not let another take you away from your path. The world is going through a big change now and in the next few years. Our advice to you is to live as simply as possible. Eliminate possessions not needed, so you can focus more on the Truth. Spend time alone each day in silence... and meditate, It is better not to have desire of this world, because everything is unimportant on that plane. It is a waste of time to accumulate riches. The kingdom of God is the real wealth, for once attained, it is never lost. You are truly loved."

* * *

Regarding HEALTH AND SURVIVAL: *"The important thing is to preserve yourself by drinking good water each day. The foods may not get better in time, but pure water will protect. All of you should be drinking more water each day."*

* * *

RELIGIOUS INSPIRATIONAL MESSAGES:

From one called Master John: *"Dear one: I know there are times that you question whether this and we are real, because you cannot see this plane. When you look at things from here you also question reality. I am as real and as unreal as yourself, for you are as much as illusion as I am. Who is to say? Who is to judge?"*

"Be the master of your own ship and love all. Do not abuse it. Take advantage of no one. You will see untruths in truth and truths in untruths. In time you will know all."

* * *

From one named Peter: *"Dear ones, I speak in behalf of the Christ. We are saddened by dissension and non-unity in the Christian churches. It will be difficult for a great master like Jesus to return to a world which is so separated by religious thoughts. We are observing those of you whose minds are more open. All spiritual books such as the Bible were written as a guide to prepare man for more loving thoughts and attitudes. But the scriptures are just the stepping stones to Truth. God is beyond words and human thoughts. We are the most content when we have gone beyond judging words. Be more like God as we were intended to be and do not get too concerned with others' thoughts and details. Be open to all great teachers. That is the best way. Jesus still loves you, and so do we."*

* * *

From the Eastern world, Lahiri Mahasaya: *"As you can see, the world has changed. It used to be that the East was much more spiritually aware than the West, but materialism is changing that. Many Americans are seeing the illusion of their material life and are going back to simplification in the spirit of God. An enlightened man does not need a church, for he is the church. Each man must seek his own path. As long as the path is one of surrender, then it is the right path; especially when self is put aside. Remember these words. All great sages are part of the One. Love all great ones so you may benefit from their teachings and blessings."*

* * *

From a monk called Shankara: *"Conserve your powers. Be like the capricious ocean, absorbing quietly all the tributary rivers of the senses, daily renewing. Sense yearnings that sap your inner peace. They are like the desert soil of materialism, the forceful, activating impulse of wrong desire. That is the greatest enemy to the happiness of man. Roam the world as a lion of self control. Don't let the throngs of sense weaken, or kick you around."*

"Destroy all wrong desires now... otherwise they will remain with you after the astral body has been separated from the physical casing. Even if the flesh is weak the mind should be constantly resistant."

* * *

From Lama Tsu Zse: *"Your help is needed. I am glad you are open to the different spiritual paths. This will enable you to receive more. I am a Buddhist monk from Tibet. You are familiar with some of my prints. Keep learning more about the Buddhist ways. You will learn true compassion, patience, humility and love for all beings. That is why you were given the 'mantra'.* **Meditation is important.** *Thank you for your contact."*

(Note: "mantra" means chants, originated from the Far East to help raise the vibration of earth.)

* * *

ABOUT JESUS

Richard asked for information about Jesus one night. A master guide brought forth the following information from the Hall of the Akashic Records, (The Akashic Records are collected from the beginning of soul memory, recorded into the spiritual realm of all wisdom):

* * *

"Jesus was a carpenter when younger, learning to build, and tear down... what His teaching was about. Building up of the spirit. Tearing down of the ego self."

"He did not desire a wife because he felt married to everyone, yet freed by them. He did not eat meat because of his love for the animal. He lived on fruits and the grains of the land."

* * *

"He was a lover of all people. He did not try to convert anyone to his way of thinking, only to their own divine way of thinking. He respected all religions and saw even the critic as an aspect of His own self; therefore, he learned at a younger age, the gift of compassion and love for All. He did not criticize others. So we must be like Him, and leave others to their own manifestation. Each will find and make his own contribution in time."

"Most of His teachings were done orally. Very little was written down. He wanted His disciples to have truths firmly planted in their minds, as well as to travel lightly. Having no possessions was having all possessions. He owned very little clothes. He loved children, reminding Him of the child within Himself, that is growing to completeness."

"Even Judas was forgiven. He did not feel resentment. Judas stayed frozen in soul for a long period of time before awakening."

* * *

"The Holy Book was written much later... after His departure. There are still enough guide lines in the book for a person to live by and be saved, for the saving is of himself and by himself."

"Jesus never felt separated from any of us. It is wise to pray to Him for we are actually praying to ourself, which is Him, in part."

"'I am the way, the Truth and the Light' was meant to be interpreted that we are the way and the truth and the light if we

would but live and follow His example as a guideline. It would simplify our life's path."

"Jesus the man will not return as many think. For His spirit is already here. There will not be one deliverer, but each will deliver himself. There will be many instrumental souls."

"Remember these words: 'Our Father, who art in heaven, Holy be Thy name. Thy Kingdom come, Thy will be done, on earth as well as in heaven.'"

"Send prayers to All things and souls, in the name of the trinity. Amen."

* * *

One night in his meditative state, Richard said, "I see Jesus. Love, spirit, not the man. Too many people love the man. I see a bright light... The sacrifice was the symbol of our soul.

"Jesus the man is not coming back, but an incarnation of God is. The people will be misled because they will be looking for Jesus the man and will look to identify with the body. It is the spirit and soul that exists, and that can take on any form."

"We must not be caught up in religious doctrines where people have a tendency to see what they want to see and interpret in only their own way. Maybe that is why I am having this vision, because I love the spirit more than the man........"

"Are my arms out? Are my ankles crossed? I feel I am on the cross!...... I feel a shaft running down the back of my neck and back.........."

* * *

"Once He merged with spirit...... no more pain...... legs feel hollow........ the illusion is physical."

* * *

"Once they cried over the body....... they lost the point... Let us think of this.........."

CHAPTER TWENTY

Beings From Outer Space

John 14:2,3:
"In my Father's house are many mansions, if it were not so, I would have told you. I go to prepare a place for you... And if I go and prepare a place for you, I will come again and receive you unto myself, that where I am, there ye may be also."

* * *

The following messages and information came from beings in a higher dimension or other planet:

* * *

"We are watching your world. It is difficult indeed. Your problem originates from your wrong thoughts and selfish desires. That is why we cannot express ourselves on your physical plane. We find it easier to communicate with your dead, for they are more in spirit than your living. Maybe perhaps someday you will see us, but only a chosen few. We and others are trying to help your world. We want to preserve it but it is difficult and we do not know how possible this will be yet. Once you are free in spirit you can see our world. You must do the best you can for ALL. Good-bye for now. ZKL."

* * *

"Dear Humans, we want you to know that we appreciate positive thoughts. You humans need to master your thoughts for they created life in themselves! This is the universal law that is known with all conscientious beings. We would like to encounter you. The thought came to us when you were in Las Vegas. It was just not in your mind that you felt that pushing to go out into the desert to meet us. We put those feelings there, and you are a very spiritual person, and one aware of the other world. You may still be taken someday. But fear not, for you will not be harmed. You will be far more harmed by your own people than by us. That is why we do not make more appearances. It would not be wise for any of us. We can change our form at will. We can look endless ways to you because we can create forms, having easily understood basic laws of this universe. Your world is wrapped in darkness. Only a few see there.

"Continue to work the best you can. Your thoughts can save your race. We would like to see all worlds in harmony. We are around. There are more around you than you ever realize. Good-bye for now... (he left no name...)

* * *

"It is very sad that we see so much potential wasted from you human beings. You have been created for an unlimited potential *but because you are a lower race you must work very hard to achieve your true potential. As you see there are always setbacks on the way, but the higher on your planet know the possibilities and can only display a small amount because of human greed and selfishness. There are many worlds such as ours who are watching, to make real contact, but the energy is not conducive to it. Remember, that there is a creative force which governs us all, in all worlds. We can see the creative force actually manifest in the physical sense, because we are more advanced.*

"*It is indeed a dark place where you are. Remember, that you cannot save everyone, so always focus on your own work first. Don't ever give up your soul growth for anything, and do not yearn for things outside of yourself. See the physical world as it is..........*"

* * *

Following the message from this being, Richard said, "He is taking me away!"

After some silence he said, "He wanted me to have this gift. He took me up and raised me out of the body. There are tangible worlds and intangible worlds... I looked down at earth... was like a blackout... hardly lit... other worlds... highly lit. Saw glimpse of the whole system. God is... and isn't... He sat me down in a seat and I watched everything... like a light force... energy... in this anything can manifest... Saw Buddha being created by light force! We need tangible creations... the force creates it. We must keep trying to improve ourselves.

From this context... the earth is the illusion... So many beings... I see why the soul struggles to go home."

* * *

Richard began to get more glimpses into other dimensions. In his next meditation he was led into another encounter:

The same being reappears. He takes Richard away, and shows him the sound of the universe.

He says, "It sounds like the fire burning, like a hot stove. Sound of flames." He adds, "I see my thought actually materialize before me. It is like a small flame that shoots into the ocean of flame. So bright just like a bright fire. Our thoughts are heard, don't you see? Heard and echoed in the great flame where all thought subsides and resides."

* * *

"Now he is showing me the way that communication is done. Same manner as they communicate with me. All thought forms all sound. Not heard with the ear, but the sound that is like the burning flame of fire."

"Now he's taking me into the dimensions of the other side of earth... yes, I see houses and environment surroundings... not solid but made of this thought. Yes, many create their own realities, but the higher, there is no house or surroundings, for they have transcended the illusory thought. It is mainly for those attached to earth life. I see some that are talking amongst themselves. Frustrated because they can't reach earth in an effective manner... so few channels. Even ones who are so-called mediums... some are not effective because they misinterpret due to their insincerity; in fact, some mediums can actually fib, which creates frustration."

* * *

"Now I'm seeing dogs and cats in the spirit world. They don't have a consciousness at all. The human thought seems to effect their karmic conditions. The more negative in the world creates greater suffering and karma for the animal kingdom. The greater the positive, these animals can transcend to higher levels which they so desperately want. Now he's taking me away..."

* * *

"This Being is nice to me... like an angel... who understands the completeness of our system. I'm asking him what is his intention. His reply is 'Only until you have completely understood your system can you ever begin to understand us and those of other worlds.' His language sounds like the 'wind' or burning fire. He's gone... I see him far away. He's waving, and my soul is shedding a tear of joy. I see the cross... and Jesus..."

* * *

"GREAT BEING"

Later on we were pleased to receive another contact from a being from outer space. He gave us no name, so we called him Great Being, G.B.

First contact: I asked, "Where are you from?"
"ALL OVER IT SEEMS."

"Have you been on earth before?"
"OH YES. I'M WHAT YOU CALL A WALK-IN."

"Oh. Then you are like a walk-in such as in Ruth Montgomery's book *Strangers Among Us*."
"OH YES. DEAR RUTH. DROP HER A LINE. SHE WILL GET A KICK OUT OF IT."

"Who shall I say contacted us?"
"JUST TELL HER A WALK-IN. BUT I AM FROM FURTHER AWAY, NOT QUITE THE SAME."

"Are you a future 'walk-in' to be on earth?"
"WALK IN, WALK OUT, WALK OUT, WALK IN. WE SPEND TIME ON EARTH AND OTHER PLACES. SOME CHOOSE TO COME BACK, OTHERS DO NOT. THERE IS A LOT OF FREE WILL AND CHOICE. THAT IS THE WHOLE POINT

FOR MAN TO LEARN TO HAVE FREE CHOICE... AND FREE WILL. MAN WILL NOT HAVE IT AS LONG AS THERE IS FIGHTING AND NEGATIVITY."

"But what you mean by walking in, is like coming into a body temporarily like with Richard?"

"YES. MANY ARE GOING THROUGH BODILY CHANGES SO THAT THIS CAN BE DONE MORE EASILY. THE BODY HAS TO MAKE PHYSICAL AND CHEMICAL CHANGES."

"Richard said he has been having bodily changes within his system for some time now. Where is he at this moment?"

"TAKING A LITTLE VACATION."

"When you are speaking through him he is out of the body?"

"YES. ANYTIME YOU ARE OUT OF THE BODY, YOU ARE TAKING A VACATION, BELIEVE ME."

"I was told that I was from Saturn; do you know if it's true?"

"IT COULD BE VERY POSSIBLE. LIFE FORMS GO ON INSIDE THE PLANETS INSTEAD OF OUTSIDE. ALSO, THE PHYSICAL IS MUCH MORE TRANSPARENT. THE HIGHER EVOLVED THE RACE THE MORE TRANSPARENT THE BODIES. THIS IS WHY YOU HAVE BEEN TAUGHT TO DEVELOP YOUR SPIRITUAL SELF. ALL THINGS THAT APPEAR TO BE SOLID ARE REALLY AN ILLUSION. ATOMS VIBRATING AT SUCH A FAST RATE YOU ONLY PERCEIVE THEM TO BE REAL, BUT ARE NOT REAL. THEY ARE ONLY YOUR PERCEPTION."

"Are you going to ever live on this planet?"
"I AM NOT SURE AT THIS POINT."

"Have you communicated with Ruth Montgomery?"

"I KNOW HER WELL, BUT HAVE NOT PERSONALLY COMMUNICATED. RUTH IS GETTING INVOLVED IN OTHER THINGS AT THIS TIME IN HER LIFE. THIS IS WHY WE NEED OTHERS SUCH AS YOURSELF TO PICK UP THE SLACK. RUTH IS TRYING TO GET MORE GROUNDED FOR NOW AND NOT PUTTING UP THE SAME AMOUNT OF TIME AND ENERGY SHE HAS BEFORE. SO WE HAVE TO LOOK FOR OTHERS TO WORK WITH AND WILL CONTINUE TO DO SO. THERE IS SO MUCH GREED AND NEGATIVITY AND SELFISHNESS IN YOUR WORLD. AND YET YOU KNOW YOUR ANSWERS. YOU PRAY TO GOD FOR ANSWERS, ASK HIGHER BEINGS SUCH AS MYSELF FOR ANSWERS, YET YOU ALREADY HAVE THE ANSWERS. YOU ALREADY KNOW THE TRUTHS. YOU KNOW THAT BY LIVING UNCONDITIONALLY THAT WILL SOLVE THE PROBLEMS, SICKNESS AND STARVATION AND ALL OTHER MALADIES IN YOUR EARTH. SO WHY KEEP ASKING, WHY NOT START DOING?"

"There are so many things we seem to want to know."

"YOU CAN KNOW MORE WHEN YOU EMPTY THE VESSEL FOR THE HIGHER. YOU WORRY ABOUT FILLING YOURSELF UP WITH A LOT OF DATA."

"Then what about writing my book?"

"YOU ARE WRITING YOUR BOOK EVERYDAY. DON'T WORRY ABOUT WHEN IT WILL BE FINISHED OR PUBLISHED. THE BOOK IS WRITING ITSELF. IT WILL ALL FALL IN PLACE IN DUE TIME."

"We want to do the right things. Humans seem to be so involved in so many things, we get entrapped. Do you see the future of us here?"

"DO YOU REALLY WANT TO KNOW THE FUTURE? OR SHOULD YOU DEAL MORE WITH THE PRESENT? YOU ALWAYS THINK THAT THE FUTURE IS GOING TO BE BET-

TER. YOU ARE ALWAYS LOOKING AHEAD FOR YOUR RAINBOWS. YET YOUR RAINBOW IS RIGHT HERE. RIGHT NOW. IT IS A MATTER OF YOUR OWN CONSCIOUS PERCEPTION. DON'T YOU SEE, IF YOU CONTINUE TO LOOK IN THE FUTURE CONSTANTLY, YOU ARE ACTUALLY CHASING A RAINBOW. YOU TRY TO CONVINCE YOURSELF THAT THERE IS SOMETHING MORE. IF I COULD JUST HAVE 'THIS' PERSON, OR JUST DO 'THIS' AND SO ON. YET EVERYTHING IS HERE."

"Do you know our relatives on the 'other' side?"

"NO, I AM SORRY I DO NOT. BUT REMEMBER, THAT THEY ARE JUST AS MUCH ALIVE AS YOU ARE. DO NOT EVER JUDGE BY YOUR LIMITED SENSES. YOUR EYES CAN ONLY SEE SO FAR. SO MANY THINGS YOU CAN NOT SEE. YOUR BODY IS A VERY BEAUTIFUL APPARATUS, BUT COMPARED TO OURS, IS VERY LIMITED."

"Do you miss a body?"

"I HAVEN'T BEEN IN A BODY AS YOU SEE IT. MINE IS MORE TRANSPARENT."

"Do you have marriages and activities similar there?"

"WE ARE NOT DIVERTED BY AS MANY INTERESTS. HERE, EVERYONE'S INTEREST IS IN SERVING THE WHOLE. THERE IS NO GREATER MISSION AND JOY THAN THAT. BECAUSE IN THIS, EXISTS ALL. INSTEAD OF FIXING OUR CARS AND WORKING, OR READING BOOKS FOR INSTANCE, WE ARE CONSTANTLY DOING THINGS IN SERVICE. YOU SHOULD DO THE LIKE. TAKE ADVICE FROM AN OLD VETERAN. YOUR REAL HAPPINESS IS THINKING ABOUT GOD, AS YOU KNOW HIM."

"Well that's fine, but we do have to worry about these physical things here, like fixing cars."

"DO NOT WORRY ABOUT THESE THINGS. THE ONLY PROBLEM IS IN YOUR MIND. WHEN THINGS GO WRONG, FIX THEM. IF SOMETHING IS WRONG WITH YOURSELF, FIX IT, BY GOING WITHIN, NOT RELYING ON OUTER SOURCES. YOU KNOW THIS TO BE TRUE, WITHIN YOURSELF."

"You mean I could mentally fix my car if I were high enough in my thinking?"

"PRECISELY. YOU WOULD KNOW WHAT THE PROBLEM WAS EXACTLY, ALL THE TIME. YOU FIX IT BY SEEING IT AS PERFECT. THOUGHT FORCE HAS MUCH POWER THAT IS FAR UNDERESTIMATED THERE."

"When you are in your vibration not having a physical body, how do you recognize other beings or souls?"

"IT IS EASIER TO RECOGNIZE THOSE HERE. WHEN YOU WALK DOWN THE STREET YOU DO NOT RECOGNIZE EVERYONE, BUT HERE EVERYONE KNOWS EVERYONE, ESPECIALLY IN THEIR ENLIGHTENED STATE, BECAUSE THERE IS NO BARRIER OR SEPARATIONS."

"How do you see them if you don't have a body with eyes?"

"SEEING IS ALL SEEING. YOU HAVE EYES, BUT YOU DO NOT SEE... YOU HAVE EARS BUT YOU DO NOT HEAR... YOU HAVE HEARD THIS BEFORE. ONE OF YOUR GREAT LEADERS HAS TOLD YOU THIS. YOU HAVE BEEN TAUGHT."

"TAP YOUR TOOLS. TAP YOUR RESOURCES. YOU HAVE THE ANSWERS. DO YOU WANT ANOTHER MATE? FINE. GET ANOTHER. WHATEVER YOU WANT, GO OUT, PLACE IT AND DO IT. BUT REMEMBER, THESE ARE ALL EXTERNAL THINGS. THEY WILL STILL NOT RECTIFY THE BASIC PROBLEM. SEE FOR YOURSELF. LOOK AT YOUR LIVES, THE WAY THEY HAVE GONE. SEE REALITY NOW. TEN

YEARS AGO YOU WERE WONDERING HOW IT WAS GOING TO BE. DON'T YOU SEE IT WILL ALWAYS BE LIKE THAT AS LONG AS YOU KEEP THE ILLUSION OF THE FUTURE BEING BETTER THAN IT IS NOW? THEN YOU WON'T BE LIVING IN THE PRESENT."

"DON'T MISS THE PRESENT MOMENT, YOUR MOMENT TO BE WITH GOD IS NOW."

"There is so much truth to that. How can we help those who have passed over into the lower, hellish realms. Just by prayer?"

"PRAYER HELPS MUCH. BUT BEING IS BETTER THAN PRAYING. IF YOU ONLY KNEW HOW YOUR CONSCIOUSNESS AFFECTS THE ENTIRE UNIVERSE. WHEN YOU STRIVE, ENDEAVOR TO UPLIFT YOURSELF, YOU BECOME A STRONGER LIGHT. AND THAT LIGHT MAKES THE UNIVERSE A BRIGHTER PLACE TO BE, WHICH MEANS ALL CAN BENEFIT, EVERYONE. THE MORE NEGATIVE YOU ARE, THE DARKER YOU ARE AND THE DARKER YOU MAKE THE UNIVERSE. REMEMBER HOW IMPORTANT YOUR PERSPECTIVE CAN BE, DAILY."

"GO BEYOND YOUR CONCEPTIONS AND JUDGMENTS, AND BECOME ONE WITH THE UNFATHOMABLE... I MUST GO. G.B."

* * *

ANOTHER MESSAGE FROM G.B.:

"IT IS SO IMPORTANT TO TAKE THIS TIME EACH DAY, EVEN IF ONLY A SMALL AMOUNT OF TIME CAN BE SPARED, TO DEVOTE UNSELFISHLY TO THE CONTRIBUTION TO THE WHOLE. YOU MUST REMEMBER, THAT NOT ONLY IS YOUR IMMEDIATE ENVIRONMENT AFFECTED, BUT OTHERS WORLDS."

"AS YOU KNOW, THE POWER, THE THOUGHT, EQUALS LIGHT, SO CONTINUE TO USE YOUR GOD ENERGY

WITHIN YOURSELVES AND YOUR THOUGHT FORMS TO MANIFEST THEM IN A BENEFICIAL WAY FOR ALL. DO NOT EVER UNDERESTIMATE YOUR POWER, ESPECIALLY THOSE PRESENT HERE TONIGHT. YOU HAVE TO BE MORE RESPONSIBLE FOR YOUR THOUGHT PROCESSES. DO NOT LET YOURSELF BE ENGULFED WITH LOW LEVELS OF NEGATIVITY, FOR YOU CAUSE MUCH REPERCUSSION TO MANY BESIDES YOURSELF."

"WITH GROWTH COMES MUCH RESPONSIBILITY. YOU MUST BE WILLING TO ACCEPT THIS RESPONSIBILITY. YOUR LIFE WILL NOT BE THE SAME. EACH DAY YOU STEP FORWARD TO MANIFEST YOUR GOD ENERGY TO MANIFEST WHO YOU REALLY ARE, YOU BECOME MORE AND MORE AWARE AND RESPONSIBLE."

"YOU MUST GIVE THOUGHT TO EVERY ACTION AND MAKE SURE NO MATTER WHAT IT IS YOU UNDERTAKE, YOU WILL NEVER HARM ANYONE, ESPECIALLY YOURSELF, FOR THERE IS NO TIME TO GO BACKWARDS. YOU MUST CONTINUE TO MOVE FORWARD. NOT ONLY ARE YOUR IMMEDIATE ONES DEPENDING ON YOU BUT WE ALL ARE."

"YOU CAN CHANGE THE VIBRATIONS OF THIS EARTH WITH YOUR OWN THOUGHT GROWTH AND PROCESS. YOUR POWER CAN HAVE SO MUCH INFLUENCE OVER OTHERS, BUT IT MUST START WITH YOU."

"TO BE A SOLAR SYSTEM THERE MUST BE A SUN TO CENTER IT. BE THAT SUN. YOU ARE SEEING OTHERS THAT ARE ADVANCED THAT ARE COMING THROUGH AT THIS TIME . DO NOT JUDGE THE PHYSICAL APPARATUS. TRY TO GET THE BENEFIT OF THE SPIRITUAL MESSAGE FROM THE ENTITIES COMING THROUGH, FOR THERE IS STILL MUCH IMPERFECTION IN THE HUMAN BEING. YOU DO NOT HAVE TIME TO EVALUATE OR JUDGE. YOU MUST TAKE WHAT YOU CAN AND GO FORWARD WITH IT."

I asked, "Where are you from?"

"I AM FROM EVERYWHERE AND NOWHERE. OUR BODIES ARE SO MUCH DIFFERENT. FORTUNATELY THEY ARE NOT AS SOLID AS YOURS. THIS IS WHY WE MAKE MUCH CONTACT WITH YOUR DECEASED. THEY CAN IDENTIFY WITH US MUCH MORE EASILY AND WE WITH THEM. HOWEVER, BECAUSE OF THE EVOLUTIONARY PROCESS OF THE ENTIRE SOLAR SYSTEM AND UNIVERSE, WE STILL HAVE TO REACH OUT TO THE HUMAN BEING IN THE PHYSICAL FORM. THE WAY THE SYSTEM IS SET UP, THE GROWTH FACTOR ACTUALLY MANIFESTS WORKING OUT THROUGH THE MATERIAL FORM."

"YOU WILL ALL TRANSCEND THE PHYSICAL AND BECOME SUCH AS I. IT IS SO MUCH MORE BENEFICIAL, FOR THERE ARE NO SELF DESIRES. THE SELF IS NO SELF. WE DO NOT HAVE HOBBIES OR HUSBANDS OR WIVES OR ANYTHING OF THAT NATURE BECAUSE WE DO NOT NEED THESE THINGS. OUR COMPLETE BEING IS THE WHOLE. THERE IS NOT ONE THING WE CAN POSSIBLY LACK. WE HAVE THE POWER TO MANIFEST WHATEVER WE WANT, TO SOLIDIFY WHAT YOU CALL MATTER. BUT IT IS A PHENOMENA THAT DOES NOT ENTERTAIN US. SO CONTINUE ON YOUR GROWTH FOR THE REWARDS ARE IMMENSE."

"ONCE YOU HAVE COMPLETED WHAT YOU CALL YOUR KARMIC CONDITIONS, AND ARE ABLE TO HAVE A CHOICE TO TRANSCEND THE PHYSICAL APPARATUS, THEN INDEED, DO SO."

I asked, "Do you ever take over a physical body when you come to earth?"

"THERE IS NO NEED TO TAKE THE TIME TO TAKE CONTROL OF THE PHYSICAL APPARATUS. THAT WOULD ONLY HINDER OUR EXPRESSION."

"WE DO TRY TO SEND LIGHT, HOPEFULLY THAT THE HUMAN SOUL WILL TUNE IN TO THIS HIGHER SOURCE. WHY SHOULD WE BURDEN OURSELVES WITH A PHYSICAL APPARATUS?"

"IT IS TIME FOR ME TO DEPART NOW. THANK YOU FOR YOUR ATTENTION. I AM HERE TO SHOW YOU THE POSSIBILITIES, WHICH ARE IMMENSE. NO MATTER WHAT YOU MAY THINK, COMPLETE ATTAINMENT AND HAPPINESS IS ON THAT PLANE WHERE THERE IS NO PHYSICAL EXTERNAL. THE PHYSICAL CAN NEVER GIVE YOU THE FREEDOM, PEACE AND COMPLETE BLISS AND JOY OF BEING COMPLETELY DISSOLVED INTO THE ONE. TRY TO ELIMINATE DESIRES. MAKE YOUR DESIRE ONE HUGE DESIRE, TO BE THAT WHICH SOMEDAY YOU WILL BE... WHAT YOU REALLY ARE... GOODBYE."

* * *

"GB" SHOWS US THE FUTURE

"I HAVE COME BACK TO HELP GIVE YOU INFORMATION FOR YOUR BOOK. YOU ARE DOING THIS WORK FOR THE GOOD OF ALL. YOU WILL BE CRITICIZED, AND YET THE ONES THAT CRITICIZE THE MOST, WANT IT THE MOST. THIS IS THE WAY OF HUMAN BEINGS. HAVE COMPASSION FOR THEM AS WELL AS YOURSELF."

"DO YOU WANT TO KNOW ABOUT THE FUTURE?"

"PEOPLE WILL NOT BE GOING TO WORK LIKE THEY ARE NOW. THEY WILL BE WORKING IN HOMES. MOST OF THE JOBS WILL BE DONE IN THE HOME. MONEY AS YOU KNOW IT WILL BE OBSOLETE. YOU WILL HAVE CARDS. CARDS THAT STICK IN A COMPUTER. BANKING WILL BE DONE AUTOMATICALLY."

"AS TIME GOES ON, THE PHYSICAL WILL BE EXERTED LESS AND THE MENTAL BODY WILL BE DOING MORE. I

DO SUGGEST THAT YOU DO NOT NEGLECT THE PHYSICAL VEHICLE. EXERCISE AND REST. THIS IS THE MISTAKE OF MANY, FOR YOU WILL GET LAZY AND NEGLECT THE PHYSICAL BODY."

"THERE WILL BE DISEASES LIKE THERE ARE NOW IF MAN CONTINUES TO THINK LIKE HE DOES NOW. THE AMOUNT OF PRAYER AND POSITIVE WORK THAT YOU AND OTHERS DO CAN HAVE AN EFFECT ON THIS, LATER."

"SEXUAL DISEASES WILL PREVAIL FOR AWHILE UNTIL THE RIGHT CONCEPTION AND IDEAS ARE MANIFESTED REGARDING THIS."

"THERE WILL BE MORE TELEPATHY DONE. IT WILL BECOME EASIER TO CONVEY AT A DISTANCE."

"THERE WILL BE MANY CULTS (GOOD AND BAD), AND SPIRITUAL LEADERS. YOU MUST USE DISCRETION AND INTUITION. IT IS TRUE THAT THINGS WILL BE MORE DIVIDED AND CLEARED; POSITIVE IN ONE AREA AND NEGATIVE IN ANOTHER, IN ORDER OF NATURE YOU MIGHT SAY."

"MANY ANIMALS WILL BECOME EXTINCT SOON UNLESS MAN PUTS OUT MORE POSITIVE ENERGY."

"THE WATER DESPERATELY NEEDS TO BE TREATED. IN FIVE YEARS IT CAN BECOME UNDRINKABLE... THE GREATEST DISASTER OF ALL!"

"WE ARE WATCHING CLOSELY. IF YOUR PLANET GETS TOO DISTRAUGHT THEN THERE WILL BE RESCUE SHIPS ARRIVING. MANY OUT OF FEAR WILL NOT ELECT TO GO, BUT THE WISE ONES WILL."

* * *

"GREAT BEING" RETURNS SOME MONTHS LATER:

He completely takes over Richard's body vehicle for the first time. Richard's eyes are closed from prayer.

"IT'S GOOD TO BE BACK. SIT DOWN. DO YOU REMEMBER ME?"

"I'm not sure," I asked, "Come closer." He was walking around.

"I AM NOT OF THIS WORLD."

"Why you are G.B!"

"YES, THAT IS WHAT YOU CALLED ME BEFORE. IT IS NOT EASY TO BE IN THIS APPARATUS. A NEW EXPERIENCE FOR ME. I DON'T KNOW HOW YOU LUG THIS THING AROUND."

"It is heavy. It is for me."

"YES, HEAVY FOR ALL OF YOU. PLEASE EVOLVE AS A RACE. IT IS SO MUCH BETTER TO BE THE OTHER WAY, TO GO LIGHTER. DO YOU REALIZE WE CAN GO THOUSANDS OF YOUR MILES IN SECONDS?"

"Wow."

"IT TAKES THE TIME WHAT YOU CALL A THOUGHT TO GO FROM ONE AREA TO ANOTHER. ONCE YOUR MIND IS COMPLETELY EVOLVED FROM YOUR SOURCE, THERE ARE NO LIMITATIONS."

"Have you been around us since the last time you came?"

"TIME IS ANOTHER ILLUSION. IT IS HARD FOR ME TO EVEN TELL YOU ABOUT TIME. IN FACT, HAVING A PHYSICAL APPARATUS THAT AGES IS HOW YOU JUDGE YOUR TIME, BUT WHEN YOU ARE NOT IN THE PHYSICAL ANYMORE YOU CAN SEE THE ILLUSIONARY DISPLAY OF IT ALL. I AM TRYING TO TALK IN A WAY THAT WILL BE EASILY UNDERSTOOD FOR YOU. THAT IS WHY I AM

USING HIS VOICE AND HIS BASIC COMMUNICATIVE PATTERNS AND HIS TERMINOLOGY. HOPEFULLY IT SOUNDS LIKE HIM."

G.B. looks around.

"YOU EVEN HAVE TO HAVE A DWELLING LIKE THIS. NOT US. THE UNIVERSE IS OUR DWELLING. HEAT, COLD, THERE IS NO SENSATION OTHER THAN THE SENSATION OF VIBRATING WITH THE SUPREME."

"YOU MUST KNOW THAT BEINGS FROM OTHER WORLDS ALL BELIEVE IN A SUPREME BEING. AND THERE ARE MILLIONS OF NAMES TO CALL IT, NAMES THAT ARE AS LONG AS ONE OF YOUR BOOKS, FROM PAGE TO PAGE. AND SHORT AS ONE OF YOUR LETTERS. BUT THERE IS NO NAME TO DESCRIBE IT, OR WORD TO PROFESS. THIS IS SOMETHING YOU MUST UNDERSTAND."

"YOU MUST GO BY YOUR EXAMPLES. YOU HAVE BEAUTIFUL BEINGS HERE. DO YOU REALIZE THAT THESE BEINGS HAVE MADE CONTACT WITH US? WHERE DID THEY GET THEIR INSPIRATION, BUT FROM HIGHER BEINGS? WE ALL ARE ON THE SAME TEAM. WE ALL ARE FIGHTING NEGATIVITY – WHICH THE NEGATIVITY ITSELF IS AN ILLUSION."

"THERE REALLY IS NO ENEMY. BUT YET THERE, IT IS VERY REAL TO YOU ON THIS EARTH, BECAUSE YOUR THOUGHTS MAKE IT REAL."

"YOUR DEVIL IS JUST AS REAL AS YOUR GOD BECAUSE OF THE THOUGHTS AND POWER YOU GIVE IT TO MANIFEST. AND THAT IS WHY. MAN SEEMS TO HAVE TO HAVE A GOOD AND BAD, OR A GOOD AND AN EVIL. YOU MUST HAVE A CONTRAST, ONE TO DEFINE THE OTHER."

"SOMEDAY HOPEFULLY YOU HUMANS WILL ALL EVOLVE AS A RACE WHERE YOU WILL SEE THE ABSURDITY; THAT IT IS NOT NECESSARY. YOU HAVE THE POWER TO TOTALLY CONTROL YOUR FATE AND DESTINY. YOU DO

NOT HAVE TO RELY ON SOMEONE ELSE. YOU SHOULD ALWAYS USE POSITIVE SPIRITUAL GUIDE LINES."

"Yes. Have there been many civilizations?"

"MANY CIVILIZATIONS. YOUR PLANET IS VERY OLD. THERE HAS BEEN VEGETATION OF THIS PLANET FOR A LONG TIME. THERE WAS TOO MUCH THOUGHT THAT CREATED YOUR PHYSICAL BEING. IT WAS ALL DERIVED FROM THOUGHT. SOME HAVE IT PARTLY RIGHT WHEN THEY SAY THAT WE DERIVED FROM THOUGHT AND THE DESIRE THAT WE WANTED TO EXPERIENCE A PHYSICAL APPARATUS. IT IS NOT NATURAL, HOWEVER. EVEN THE DIVISION ITSELF IS NOT NATURAL, OF MALE AND FEMALE. IT ONLY SEEMS SO."

"I see. Is our planet really threatened by destruction?"

"THREATENED BY YOUR OWN THOUGHTS, THAT IS THE ONLY THING THAT THREATENS IT, YOUR OWN COLLECTIVE THINKING. FOR IT WAS YOUR OWN COLLECTIVE THINKING THAT STARTED IT IN THE FIRST PLACE. CERTAINLY DO NOT BLAME IT ON GOD OR A DEVIL."

"WELL, I THINK I WILL SIT THIS THING DOWN. (He sits) DO NOT TOUCH ME. I THINK I WILL SEND THOUGHTS OF GRATITUDE THAT I DO NOT HAVE THIS CONTRAPTION TO STAY AROUND ME."

"And people here are afraid of transferring to another realm, or dying."

"I WOULD WELCOME IT IF I HAD TO LIVE IN THIS. (He laughs) YOU WILL FEEL INVIGORATED WHEN YOU DO LEAVE YOUR BODY."

"All don't do they? Don't some go to the lower realms in their negativity?"

"ONLY IN THOUGHTS. YOU ONLY MANIFEST WHAT YOU THINK."

"But prayer does help those unhappy souls.?"

"PRAYER IS THE ONLY THING THAT HELPS THE SOUL'S ENERGY. THOUGHT AND WHAT YOU CALL ENERGY ARE SYNONYMOUS. YOUR MIND CAN BE A VERY VOLATILE TOOL. THE MIND MUST BE QUIETED DOWN AND DIRECTED. LIKE WHAT YOU WOULD CALL TAMING ONE OF YOUR HORSES. YOUR AVERAGE MIND IS LIKE A WILD HORSE, SO YOU NEVER GET THE FULL BENEFIT OF YOUR LIFE IN THE BODY. IT IS LIKE YOU ARE ALWAYS CHASING YOUR WILD HORSE. BUT IF YOU TAMED YOUR HORSE, AND THIS IS WHAT YOUR SO-CALLED SPIRITUAL DISCIPLINES ARE TRYING TO GET YOU TO DO, THEN YOU CAN REALLY TAKE ADVANTAGE OF THE POWER THAT YOU REALLY HAVE. YOUR GREAT ONES ARE THOSE THAT HAVE REALIZED THIS AND DIRECTED THEIR ENERGY WITH THEIR MINDS AND ALSO DEVOTED THE FRUITS OF THEIR ACTIONS FOR ALL OF US."

"But we have to make a living and worry about mundane things here it seems. It takes us away from it just trying to survive."

"I UNDERSTAND. IT IS UNFORTUNATE. BUT YOU STILL MUST REALIZE THAT YOU WILL NOT BE IN THE BODY PERMANENTLY, SO WHY NOT FOCUS ON THE THINGS THAT ARE PERMANENT?"

"Are you directing that to Richard and me?"

"IT IS FOR ALL TO HEAR, AND DO. GOODBYE FOR NOW..."

* * *

"The UFO phenomenon is a challenge to mankind. It is the duty of scientists to take up this challenge, to disclose the nature of the UFO and to establish the scientific truth."

Dr. Felix Zigel, Moscow Institute of Aviation

CHAPTER TWENTY ONE

Questions to the Other Side

The following questions, I asked from guides and loved ones, and higher intelligence from beyond. I would like to share their answers.

* * *

PERSONAL QUESTIONS

When I found out that my guide, RX, was also my husband Matt in a past lifetime from the early West, I wanted to know, did he "see" me as I look now, or as I looked then?

Matt responded:

"I AM SEEING YOU THE WAY I WISH TO SEE YOU, THE WAY I REMEMBER YOU, YOUNG, WITH LONG DARK HAIR, FOR I DO NOT SEE THE PHYSICAL WAY YOU PERCEIVE YOURSELF (I am now in my fifties and blonde).

WHEN YOU CROSS OVER YOU WILL SEE ME AS I PROJECTED IN THAT LIFETIME. EVEN THOUGH THE FORM ITSELF IS AN ILLUSION AN A PROJECTION OF THE PAST, IT APPEARS REAL."

I replied, "In other words, you can project yourself in any way you wish to Richard?"

"THAT IS RIGHT."

* * *

I asked Matt another time, "Since I was married to you and my husband from this time has passed over, are there jealousies there to deal with?

"WHAT IS THERE TO BE JEALOUS OF? WE ARE ALL THE SAME. THAT IS WHY IT IS EASY TO STAND BACK AND LET YOUR HUSBAND JASON COME FORWARD SO MUCH INSTEAD OF MYSELF. HE IS MUCH NEWER HERE AND NOT AS DETACHED. HE IS LEARNING FAST THE IMPORTANCE OF DETACHED LOVE."

* * *

QUESTIONS TO MY FATHER:

"Dad, do you live in a house there and live like we do, around material objects?"

"NO. I AM MORE FREE. I USED TO."

"Is it better for you now than before?" I remembered his many unhappy times and fears before he died.

"WHEN YOU ARE LEARNING AND ADVANCING, IT IS MUCH BETTER. YOU MUST BE OPEN TO LEARNING SO MANY THINGS. A HOUSE WOULD ONLY CONFINE YOUR ENVIRONMENT I DON'T NEED THAT FALSE SENSE OF SECURITY LIKE MANY OTHERS HERE."

"Do you ever sleep anymore?"

"YES A LOT AT THE BEGINNING, BUT NOT SO MUCH NOW. MOST OF THE TIME IS LEARNING. IF YOU ONLY KNEW HOW MUCH THERE IS TO LEARN."

"Being closed minded here on earth about the hereafter really holds one back, doesn't it?"

"YES. IT CERTAINLY DOES. MOST PEOPLE CROSS OVER WITH THEIR LIMITED THOUGHTS ABOUT REALITY, SO THEY ARE CONFINED AS TO THE RESULT. BUT PRAYERS THROW LIGHT TO THE WAY. IT IS LIKE PUTTING GLASSES ON WHEN YOU HAVE POOR VISION. EACH ONE GOES AT HIS OWN PACE WHEN THEY COME OVER. SOME SLEEP A LONGER TIME. EVEN WHEN FIRST MADE CONTACT WITH YOU I STILL TRIED TO SLEEP A LOT FOR THE MOST PART. I KEPT REACHING BACK TO YOU BECAUSE I FELT THE NEED TO HELP YOU UNDERSTAND MORE; AND BECAUSE YOU WERE SO OPEN, WE BOTH PROGRESSED. NOW I AM MORE FREE TO PURSUE MY SCHOOLING."

"Is it like going to class there?"

"YES AND NO. IT IS NOT LIKE A CLASSROOM. MORE PERSONAL. MORE LIKE AN EVALUATION, AND A LEARNING OF TRUTHS."

"Do you have companionship there?"

"IT IS NOT AS IMPORTANT WHEN YOU ARE OUT OF THE BODY. YOU HAVE IT WHEN YOU WANT IT."

* * *

QUESTIONS TO MY MOTHER, PATRICIA:

"Mother, Can you see yourself back the way you were in other lifetimes?"

"I HAVE MEMORY FLASHES. SOME CAN DO THIS, OTHERS NOT. IT IS EASIER ACTUALLY TO REMEMBER WHEN YOU ARE STILL IN THE BODY, BECAUSE YOU ARE ALWAYS REINCARNATED IN THE BODY, AND BEING THERE CAN REMIND YOU OF BEING IN FORMER BODIES."

"I see. So with training we can tap in and remember our own past lives while we are still here?"

"YES. WE MAY CONFER WITH A HIGHER SOUL TO HELP US, AND ALSO INFORMATION IS HERE IN THE AKASHIC RECORDS. YOU MAY LEARN TO TAP INTO YOUR SUBCONSCIOUS WHERE ALL YOUR MEMORY IS."

"When we wish to make a contact with someone departed, is it easier for them to come through on a Ouija board, automatic writing, or direct, like through Richard?"

"IT IS EASIER THROUGH THE MIND, FOR IN ALL OTHER METHODS THERE ARE PHYSICAL OBJECTS INVOLVED."

"There can be interferences with that?"
"YES."

"Can you come in dreams to us?"
"YES WE CAN."

"Have you contacted me in my dreams?"
"YES MANY TIMES"

"It's too bad I can't always remember, only a few times."
"IT IS THE SAME HERE. THERE IS MUCH WE DO NOT REMEMBER, FOR IT IS NOT FOR DWELLING ON THE

PAST, BUT FOR PREPARATION OF THE FUTURE, ON THIS LEVEL."

"Do you know when you are going to incarnate again on earth or anything about your next time?"

"YES, I WILL BE A WOMAN AGAIN. I WILL HAVE A TOTALLY DIFFERENT WAY AND PERSONALITY. I WILL BE QUIET, NOT AS ASSERTIVE. BUT IT IS WHAT IS NEEDED."

"Do you know who you will be associated with next time?"

"I AM STILL IN THE PROCESS OF DETERMINING THE CIRCUMSTANCES."

"Who helps you formulate this, a high master, God, or yourself?"

"YES, THEM ALL. IT IS ALL THE SAME."

"Are you on a different plane or level there than Sandy, your last husband, or my dad?"

"I AM IN THE THIRD DIMENSION, SAME AS YOUR FATHER. I COMMUNICATE WITH HIM MORE THAN SANDY BECAUSE WE ARE IN THE SAME DIMENSION. SANDY HAS NOT YET REACHED THIS DIMENSION."

"Can you help bring Sandy up to a higher dimension by sending him light?"

"HE WILL BE HELPED THE MORE HE DESIRES TO RECEIVE IT."

"Is the lower, or astral plane the first dimension?"

"THE FIRST DIMENSION IS LIKE A HELL REALM, THE SECOND REALM HAS CONFUSION BUT IS IMPROVED. MY DIMENSION IS THE ONE OF DESIRE."

"Human desires or spiritual desires?"

"BOTH. BETWEEN THE EARTH PULLINGS AND THE SPIRITUAL UPLIFTING WE ARE IN THE REALM AND PLACE WE HAVE CREATED FOR OURSELVES."

"But doesn't it help to send him light and love?"

"YES IT ALWAYS HELPS, IT IS THE BEST HELP WE CAN DO. BUT HE HAS TO DESIRE IT. UNFORTUNATELY, LIKE SO MANY OTHERS, HE IS IN A REALM OF IGNORANCE, BUT IS LEARNING TO WORK WITH HIS SOUL NEEDS. WHEN THAT IS ACCOMPLISHED THEN HE WILL GO THE DESIRE REALM. REMEMBER WHETHER ONE IS ON YOUR SIDE, OR THIS SIDE ONE MUST HAVE THE MOTIVATION FOR HIGHER LEARNING"

"Since you have been a guide to us, and especially Annette, and from the third dimension, can our upsets pull you down, or uplift your strength by helping?"

"IT IS LIKE YOU TRYING TO HELP YOUR DAUGHTER, VIKEE. YOU HAVE A DESIRE TO HELP HER, BUT YOU MAY NOT BE ABLE TO TELL HER ALL THE RIGHT THINGS. IN OTHER WORDS YOUR INFORMATION CAN GET CONFUSED THE SAME AS MINE. ONE IS NOT ALWAYS AWARE OF WHAT IS BEST FOR HER SOUL GROWTH BECAUSE OF LIMITED PERSPECTIVE. YOUR DESIRE FOR YOUR DAUGHTER'S HAPPINESS CAN EITHER BE BETTER FOR YOU BECAUSE YOU ARE SINCERELY TRYING TO HELP ANOTHER, OR WORSE FOR YOU BECAUSE YOU MAY GET CAUGHT UP IN HER EMOTIONS WANTING HER TO BE HAPPY, SO IT DEPENDS ON YOUR LEVEL AND HOW YOU WORK WITH IT, SAME AS WITH ME."

"Mother, when I want to communicate with you again, how will I know when you are around?"

"USE YOUR MIND. DIRECT YOUR ENERGY. IT IS LIKE TURNING YOUR TV ON AND DIRECTING TO ONE CHANNEL. THAT'S WHAT A CHANNELER DOES, TUNE IN."

"Do our guides keep negative spirits and influences away from us, or is it all up to us?"

"IT IS MOSTLY UP TO YOU. THE IMPORTANT THING HERE IS TO ACKNOWLEDGE THAT NEGATIVE SPIRITS ARE AROUND. IT IS NOT A MATTER OF KEEPING THEM AWAY, FOR THAT IS REINFORCING THEIR REALTY. BE AWARE OF THEM, BUT ALSO ACKNOWLEDGE THAT THEY ARE ONLY THERE IN YOUR MIND. WHEN YOU ARE FEELING ANYTHING OTHER THAN HAPPY AND CONTENT, REALIZE YOU ARE ACTUALLY TUNING IN TO THE LOWER ENERGY."

"SO, TURN THE CHANNEL. IF YOU DO NOT LIKE WHAT YOU ARE WATCHING ON TELEVISION, WHAT DO YOU DO, VIKEE?"

"I just turn the channel over."

"THERE YOU GO. AND I WILL LEAVE YOU WITH THAT."

"Mother. Just one more question. You were sixty-two when you passed over. Was that the time that was planned for you to leave?"

"DEAR, I LEFT EARTH A LOT EARLIER THAN PLANNED BECAUSE I OVER DID IT AND LET OTHERS UPSET ME. I LET STRESS TAKE OVER, THUS MY STROKE. SO, PLEASE TAKE CARE OF YOURSELF SO YOU MAY LIVE OUT YOUR INTENDED LONG LIFE."

"I WILL BE AROUND MY DEAR, ESPECIALLY WHEN YOU NEED ME."

* * *

QUESTIONS TO GUIDES:

"What is it like when one passes over?"

"IT IS SO IMPORTANT NOT TO BE AFRAID AND NEGATIVE WHEN PASSING OVER, FOR MANY WHO ARE IGNORANT AND UNEVOLVED IT IS LIKE BEING THROWN INTO A PITCH DARK ROOM. IT IS MOSTLY SLEEP. EVEN WHEN YOU THINK YOU ARE AWAKE IT IS LIKE YOU ARE ASLEEP. THERE CAN BE A SENSE OF DESPERATION. BUT PRAYER IS LIKE A BEAM OF LIGHT COMING INTO THE DARK ROOM, WHICH GIVES HOPE AND INSPIRATION. SEEING THE LIGHT ENCOURAGES ONE TO GET OUT OF THE DARKNESS WHICH THEY CAN AS SOON AS THEY DESIRE TO."

"DEATH IS ALWAYS AROUND THE CORNER. IT IS LIFE'S MOST AWESOME EVENT, AND BECAUSE YOU NEVER KNOW WHEN IT WILL ACTUALLY OCCUR, IT IS SPIRITUALLY PARAMOUNT THAT YOU MAKE PREPARATIONS FOR YOUR INEVITABLE TRANSITION. EVERYONE'S LIFE IS SUBJECT TO DANGER AS LONG AS PREPARATIONS HAVE NOT BEEN MADE."

"What does death mean?"

"WHEN A SOUL FIRST PASSES OVER IT IS GENERALLY A SHOCK TO THE AVERAGE SOUL. AT FIRST THERE IS NO REACTION. AFTER THE ENTITY HAS ADJUSTED THEN THEY REACT ACCORDING TO WHERE THEY ARE WITH THEIR KARMA AND SPIRITUAL DEVELOPMENT. SOME WILL CLING WITH FEAR, WHILE OTHERS WILL FEEL RELIEVED OF THE GREAT BURDENS ON EARTH. A GREAT, LOVING FORCE DECIDES WHAT IS BEST FOR THE INDIVIDUAL SOUL. EVERYONE IS PACED DIFFERENTLY. SOME WILL REST, WHILE OTHERS WILL START MAKING PREPARATION FOR THE NEXT ROUND. THE SOUL THAT IS A SPIRITUAL SEEKER SEES THE CYCLE OF DEATH AND REBIRTH AND PRAYS TO ENLIGHTEN THEMSELVES AS SOON AS POSSIBLE."

"Do those that have just passed over feel any pain?"

"NOT IN A PHYSICAL SENSE, BUT IN A SPIRITUAL OR MENTAL SENSE, ACCORDING TO THEIR CONSCIOUSNESS OF BEING POSITIVE."

"Can one die before 'planned'?"

"YES, ESPECIALLY WHEN IGNORANCE AND DIVERSION FROM THE SPIRITUAL, AND NEGATIVITY IS INVOLVED. THEN LIFE HAS A HARD TIME RESUMING IT'S NATURAL COURSE OF EVENTS, SO MAKE ACQUAINTANCE WITH GOD NOW."

"After one passes over, is there a set time when they reincarnate, or return to earth?"

"THERE IS NO SET RULE AS TO WHEN YOU REINCARNATE. BUT IT CAN BE PROLONGED, DUE TO KARMIC ACCUMULATION AND ACCORDING. IT IS A PRECIOUS THING TO HAVE A HUMAN FORM AND TO WORK WITH A BODY. TAKE CARE OF IT SO YOU CAN GET ON WITH YOUR WORK. THERE CAN BE NO GAIN WITH A BODY FILLED WITH PAIN."

"AS THE DIMENSIONS INCREASE, THE COMMUNICATION BETWEEN SOULS BECOMES MORE SUBTLE, EVEN AS WE KNOW IT PHYSICALLY, AND IS ELIMINATED AS WE EXPAND IN THE DIMENSIONS. THERE IS NO SET TIME, PAST, PRESENT OR FUTURE. ALL CAN BE KNOWN AT ANY MOMENT, FOR THINGS ARE AS THEY ARE. SHUT OUT NEGATIVITY. CONTROL IT, SO THAT YOU MAY NOT HARM OTHERS."

"Will animals reincarnate?"

"ANIMALS COME FROM COLLECTIVE CONSCIOUSNESS. AFTER A SERIES OF ROUNDS THE ANIMAL WILL TRANSFORM INTO ANOTHER ANIMAL BUT NOT A HUMAN BEING AS WE KNOW IT. THERE IS STILL MORE TO LEARN HERE."

"What about eating animals?"

"IT IS NOT SO WRONG TO EAT FISH BECAUSE THERE ARE SO MANY, BUT IT IS MUCH DIFFERENT WITH CATTLE. THERE, LIFE GOES ON IN THE MILK. IT IS BETTER TO ABSTAIN FROM EATING THE FLESH."

"Can animals progress mentally?"

"THE GENERAL ATMOSPHERE IS A POSITIVE AND HARMONIOUS ONE. THE ANIMALS WILL PROGRESS MORE COLLECTIVELY THAN INDIVIDUALLY. AGAIN, POSITIVE THINKING AND PRAYERS NOT ONLY ELEVATE THIS WORLD BUT IN LOWER WORLDS, AS THE ANIMALS, PLANTS AND SO ON."

"Can another spirit body intermingle with a physical body?"

"IT IS NOT NATURAL TO INTERMINGLE IN A BODY AND CAN PRODUCE DIFFICULTIES; THEREFORE, FOR TRUE AND MOST EFFECTIVE COMMUNICATION IT SHOULD BE DONE BY RAISING THE VIBRATION AND TUNING IN TO THE SPIRIT. IN THE CASE OF A MEDIUM, WHEN THE BODY IS TAKEN OVER BY ANOTHER, YOU LOSE CONSCIOUSNESS TO SOME DEGREE. BUT BY BRINGING YOUR CONSCIOUSNESS UP TO A HIGHER LEVEL THE SAME CAN BE ACCOMPLISHED IN COMMUNICATION AND MUCH MORE SAFELY, AS RICHARD DOES."

"Then the methods of the medium and the channeler are the same?"

"IT IS IMPORTANT TO UNDERSTAND THAT EVERYTHING IS CHANGING AND IS IMPERMANENT ON YOUR PLANET SO THEREFORE, DOES IT REALLY MATTER WHAT STEP EACH IS ACTUALLY GOING THROUGH? IT ONLY MATTERS HOW EACH IS SPIRITUALLY GROWING AND REACHING OUT TO FEEL THE ONE NESS AS THE OTHER DIMENSION IS TAPPED."

"REMEMBER THAT THE REASON WHY CONTACTS CAN BE MADE WITH BEINGS OUTSIDE OF YOURSELF IS A REMINDER THAT THERE IS NO INHERENT SEPARATION, ONLY THE ILLUSION OF SEPARATENESS. THEREFORE, YOU CAN BE AT ONE... DEPENDING ON YOUR EXPANSION AND LOVE FOR ALL."

"THINGS ARE CHANGING RAPIDLY ON EARTH, EVEN METHODS OF CONTACT. AS YOU REMEMBER YOUR FIRST CONTACT WAS MORE AN EXCHANGE OF SOULS. BUT THAT WAS THEN, AND AS MAN DEVELOPS WITH TECHNOLOGY HE ALSO CAN DEVELOP SPIRITUALLY. AS A CAR, SO A PLANE. AS A SLOWER CONTACT, THEN A MORE EVOLVED ONE, SUCH AS YOUR FIRST EXPERIENCE, IN CONTRAST TO NOW."

"Can anyone do what Richard is doing in spirit communication?"

"IT CAN BE DONE BY TRUE SPIRITUAL SEEKERS AND THOSE RAISING THEIR VIBRATION. EACH HAS THEIR OWN SPECIAL GIFTS."

"IN SUMMARY, AS THE SOUL GROWS SO DOES THE METHODS OF CONTACT SINCE THE RACE HAS EVOLVED, SOMEWHAT BEING MORE OPEN TO THIS NOW, IT IS MUCH MORE FREQUENT TO CONTACT IN THIS MANNER, VERSUS THE OLD WAY, EVEN THOUGH IT IS STILL DONE."

"Then a man cannot be possessed another entity unless he agrees to it?"

"IT IS VERY UNLIKELY THAT ANOTHER SOUL CAN TAKE OVER THE BODY UNLESS THERE IS SOME FAILURE ALONG THE LINE. NO ONE ENTITY CAN TOTALLY POSSESS ANOTHER; HOWEVER, MANY ARE INFLUENCED BY THE SURROUNDING CONSCIOUSNESS THAT IS BEING DRAWN TO THAT INDIVIDUAL. THIS IS WHY IT IS SO IM-

PORTANT TO THINK POSITIVE AND TO BE IN A POSITIVE ENVIRONMENT. THINK LOVE, SEND OUT LIGHT. GIVING LOVE CAN ONLY RESULT IN RECEIVING LOVE."

"But if in agreement, is it okay for spirit exchange?"

"ONLY FOR A SHORT PERIOD. IT IS NOW NOT NECESSARY TO COMMUNICATE IN THIS MANNER, AS WE NO LONGER NEED BUGGIES NOW THAT WE HAVE CARS, DO YOU SEE?"

"Is it because it is dangerous?"

"IT IS MORE DIFFICULT FOR EFFECTIVENESS, SO WHY TRANSFER THE SOUL TO DIFFERENT PLANES WHEN IT IS NOT NECESSARY. SUCH AS WHY WALK TO THE NEXT TOWN TO VISIT A FRIEND WHEN YOU CAN JUST CONTACT THEM BY PHONE?"

"CONTINUE YOUR WORK AND SEND OUT LOVE AND LIGHT. DO NOT WORRY ABOUT THE DIFFERENCES, FOR THERE WILL ALWAYS BE THOSE. THE KEY WILL BE RAISING OF THE COLLECTIVE CONSCIOUSNESS SO THAT ALL DIFFERENCES WILL ONLY COMPLIMENT EACH OTHER THROUGH UNIVERSAL MEDITATION, REAL LOVE AND COMPASSION."

"What about using the Ouija board for contacts?"

"WHEN YOU GET MESSAGES FROM A OUIJA BOARD IT IS USUALLY FROM THE FIRST DIMENSION AND YOU CAN NOT RELY ON THAT DIMENSION ANY MORE THAN THE EARTH PEOPLE. REMEMBER THAT EVEN WHEN YOUR LOVED ONES ARE SPEAKING, IT IS LIKE TALKING TO A NEIGHBOR, SO KEEP THAT IN MIND."

"YOUR GUIDES SUCH AS K.W. AND FRIENDS FROM ABOVE ARE IN THE HIGHER DIMENSION, USUALLY THE FOURTH PLANE. FOR BETTER GUIDANCE PRAY THAT YOU WILL BE OPEN TO THE HIGHER PLANS SUCH A THESE."

"WE KNOW WHAT IS GOING ON EVEN WHEN WE ARE NOT IN ATTENDANCE SO REMEMBER, THAT PRAYERS AND POSITIVE THOUGHTS ARE NEVER WASTED. WORRIES AND POSSESSIVENESS ARE NEGATIVE. YOU MUST NEVER FORCE. LET ANOTHER DO WHAT THEY MUST."

"Why can't we always get a response from someone on the other realm that we are trying to reach?"

"WHEN YOU HAVE GONE OVER TO THE OTHER SIDE SOMETIMES YOU MAY FIND IT HARD TO MAKE A CONTACT WITH ONE FAMILIAR TO YOU. THIS IS BECAUSE THE SOUL HAS DEEPER ATTACHMENTS IN CONNECTIONS TO OTHERS. SO, IF A RELATIVE CANNOT BE REACHED THEN EITHER THE SOUL HAS GONE INTO A DEEP SLEEP, A DIFFERENT DIMENSION OR REALM, OR HAS REINCARNATED, OR JUST DOES NOT WISH TO RESPOND BECAUSE OF ANOTHER INVOLVEMENT AT THAT TIME. SOMETIMES A SOUL MAY CHOOSE TO RELEASE HIS IDENTITY IN THAT PARTICULAR LIFE IN WHICH YOU HAVE IDENTIFIED HIM."

"WHEN YOU PRAY FOR THIS SOUL, PRAY FOR HIS HAPPINESS, NO MATTER WHICH CHOICE HE HAS TAKEN. THE LIBERATED BEING IS FROM ALL DIMENSIONS. THE HIGHER UP YOU GO, THE LESS THE EXPANSION BETWEEN PLACES. IN EACH DIMENSION THAT YOU GRADUATE TO, YOU BECOME A NEW DIMENSION PLUS THE LAST ONE."

"Was there really a Lucifer or Devil?"

"YES AND NO. DEPENDS ON YOUR OWN CONCEPT OF WHAT IS REAL. ANYTHING IS REAL IF YOU REINFORCE IT. HOW A PERSON SEES THIS DOES NOT MAKE THEM RIGHT OR WRONG. FOR TRUE GROWTH IT IS MUCH WISER NOT TO BELIEVE IN THE CONCEPT OF THE DEVIL, FOR IT CAN REINFORCE FEELINGS OF SEPARATENESS AND FEAR. GO BEYOND YOUR CONCEPT OF

LIMITED MIND. BUT FOR THE ONES WHO MANIFEST THIS THEY CREATE NEGATIVE PATTERNS THAT ARE ABSORBED BY MANY ON EARTH. IT IS EASIER TO BE NEGATIVE THAN POSITIVE BECAUSE OF OUR BASIC SUFFERING AND SEPARATIONS. AS WE FEEL OUR ONENESS WITH THE DIVINE WE ELIMINATE OUR FEARS AND SEPARATENESS."

"This New age has brought many channelers to the surface, such as Ramtha, Lazarus, etc. Through some unfavorable publicity the validity of these beings have been questioned as well as the integrity of the one channeling because of the material gain."

"THERE IS NOTHING WRONG WITH THE ENTITIES. IT IS NOT A FAULT OF AN ENTITY IF THE CHANNELER CANNOT KEEP THINGS UNDER CONTROL. THE TEACHINGS ARE GOOD. THERE WILL BE MANY OF THESE TO COME IN FUTURE YEARS. ALL WILL BE SLIGHTLY DIFFERENT SO THAT THE PEOPLE WILL HAVE CHOICE, JUST AS THERE ARE MORE THAN ONE CHOICE OF CHURCHES TO ATTEND. THE ESSENCE WILL WORK OUT TO BE THE SAME IN THE LONG RUN."

"HOWEVER, THE CHANNELER HAS A TREMENDOUS RESPONSIBILITY TO REMAIN HUMBLE AND TO KEEP THINGS IN A HARMONIOUS EXPRESSION. THEREFORE, THE TRUE CHANNELER OR SPIRITUAL DEVOTEE MUST KEEP HIMSELF IN CHECK AT ALL TIMES IN ORDER TO GUARANTEE THE RIGHT MESSAGES, WHICH MUST BE EGOLESS ON BOTH THE SPIRITUAL AND PHYSICAL APPARATUS. WE HOPE THAT ALL WHO ARE ENGAGED IN THIS WORK WILL HEED THESE WORDS AND LEARN FROM THIS EXPERIENCE, FROM THE RECENT UNFAVORABLE CRITICISM."

"IN REGARD TO THE CHANNELER OF RAMTHA AS REFERRED TO FROM THE TELEVISION REPORT, SHE MAY HAVE LOST SOME BALANCE BECAUSE OF THE EXCESS OF MATERIAL GAIN WHICH IS CAUSING HER ANXIETY, IN-

STEAD OF BEING CONTENT TO BE OF MORE SIMPLICITY AND HAVE FEWER THINGS. HER MOTIVE MAY HAVE BEEN FOR THE GOOD, AND NOW SHE HAS THE BURDEN AND ANXIETY OF TRYING TO MAINTAIN AND HOLD ONTO SUCH EXCESS, AS DO SO MANY OTHERS. WHEN THE MIND IS PRE-OCCUPIED WITH MUNDANE AND PULLING MATTERS, HOW CAN THE WHOLE SYSTEM NOT BE AFFECTED?"

"PROSPERITY, IS PEACE OF MIND IN EXPANSION OF THE SPIRIT. THESE THINGS ARE NOT LOST. NOTHING STAYS PERMANENT IN THE MATERIAL WORLD. HOWEVER, TRUTHS ARE TRUTHS."

"Are there what is called Soul Mates?"

"THERE IS NOT JUST ONE PERSON FOR ONE. WHEN YOU HAVE DISSOLVED YOUR SEPARATENESS YOU WILL HAVE NO NEED, BECAUSE THERE WILL NOT BE A NEED. TRUE, SOME SOULS ARE BETTER SUITED FOR YOU, DEPENDING ON THE PERSONALITY YOU ARE PORTRAYING, BUT IN TRUTH, WHAT MAY BE IDEAL NOW WILL BE DIFFERENT LATER."

"While we are on earth, is it wrong to think you have a Twin Soul?"

"GO WITH WHAT I JUST SAID. IT IS NOT WRONG, BUT AGAIN, YOU MUST LOOK AT WHAT YOU ARE DOING BY WANTING OR DESIRING SOMEONE IN ADDITION TO YOURSELF. ARE YOU NOT JUST REINFORCING YOUR OWN ILLUSION OF DEPENDENCY AND SEPARATENESS? THINK ABOUT THIS. IF YOU REALLY WANT TO STRIVE FOR COMPLETE SPIRITUAL ENLIGHTENMENT THEN GO BEYOND. DO NOT GRASP OR DESIRE OTHER THAN THIS."

"Then again, it is wrong to even desire a mate?"

"IT IS NOT WRONG TO DESIRE A MATE. BUT REMEMBER, EVERYTHING REMAINS IMPERMANENT ON YOUR PLANE. SO MOST SOULS END UP CREATING MORE ATTACHMENT AND KARMA BY PURSUING COMPANIONSHIP IN THIS WAY. ONLY WHEN YOU ARE SPIRITUALLY BALANCED CAN YOU TRULY REAP THE REWARDS OF COMPANIONSHIP. OTHERWISE, DISAPPOINTMENT AND PAIN WILL DETER FROM PEACE AND HARMONY."

"If you think you are not with your soul (or right) mate, should you look around and seek your compatible one?"

"WHEN YOU ARE UNHAPPY. WHERE CAN YOU GO THAT YOUR UNHAPPINESS WILL NOT FOLLOW? FIRST DISSOLVE YOUR CONCEPTIONS OF REALITY, REALIZING IT IS ALL TEMPORARY."

"Yes, but with some souls we feel more harmonious with to progress with. Is that all in the mind?"

"IT IS TRUE THERE IS A CLOSER ASSOCIATION VERSUS OTHERS. MORE OF A FEELING OF A LIFETIME SHARING CONNECTION. BUT ULTIMATELY THIS WILL ALL GO. YOU WILL EVENTUALLY SEE THE PART YOU ARE PLAYING IN EACH LIFETIME FOR WHAT IT IS, AND YOU WILL NOT FEEL THE CLINGING, OR BE IN THE ILLUSION ANY LONGER."

"Then we should release the whole idea of soul mates and seeking the right one?"

"THINK ABOUT DOING YOUR OWN WORK AND BE OPEN TO YOUR LIFE. IF YOU CAN PEACEFULLY SHARE IT WITH ANOTHER, FINE, BUT ONE DAY REFLECT AND KNOW THAT YOUR ASSOCIATION IS ONLY TEMPORARY. IN THIS STATE, GOING BEYOND THE NEED... YOU WILL NEVER FEEL LONELY"

"Wasn't the soul originally split? (half male and half female)?"

"ANSWER NO. ANSWER YES. BECAUSE IT WAS LATER THOUGHT THAT THE SOUL'S MODE OF HUMAN EXPRESSION COULD EXPAND AND ACCELERATE AT A FASTER RATE IF IT HAD A CHOICE BETWEEN SEXES. BUT IF YOU GO BACK TO THE ORIGINAL CONCEPT THAT THERE IS INHERENTLY NO SEPARATENESS, THEN THE SOUL IS NEITHER MALE OR FEMALE IN TRUTH. THEN THE WHOLE IDEA OF SOUL MATES CAN ONLY BE A TEMPORARY EXPRESSION AND WILL, UNTIL YOU HAVE DISSOLVED YOUR "SEPARATENESS". SO YOU SHOULD NOT BE CONCERNED ABOUT BEING AN IDEAL MAN OR WOMAN, BUT A BALANCED BEING."

"TIMES ARE DIFFERENT, AND YET YOU ARE LUCKY TO BE LIVING IN A PERIOD WHICH ENABLES YOU TO EXPERIENCE BOTH SIDES, MALE AND FEMALE OF YOUR BEING. DO NOT JUDGE OTHERS IN THIS RESPECT. BE YOUR OWN DIVINE SPARK. ILLUMINATE SO THAT ALL CAN SEE YOUR LIGHT, REGARDLESS OF WHICH SEX YOU ARE."

"Can prayers keep the earth from being destroyed?"

"YES. THERE IS A LOT OF PREPARATION GOING ON TO HELP RECONSTRUCT EARTH AND IT VIBRATIONS. DO NOT BE LIMITED BY WHAT YOU SEE OR HEAR. THE ANSWERS ARE BEYOND THE SENSES."

"What about another world war?"

"STILL IN QUESTION AT THIS POINT. IF YOU PEOPLE CAN UNITE SPIRITUALLY AND SUSTAIN YOUR EFFORT, THEN IT CAN BE AVOIDED. BUT REMEMBER, ANOTHER WORLD WILL BE CREATED AND IT WILL ALL START OVER, SO WHAT IS THE POINT? WHY NOT SETTLE HERE AND NOW. THINK PEACE, FEEL PEACE, AND PRAY FOR PEACE."

"Will Russia become peaceful?"

"THIS COUNTRY IS VERY NEGATIVE BECAUSE THEY KNOW SUBCONSCIOUSLY THAT THEY ARE DOING A NEGATIVE THING BY DENYING PEOPLE AND COUNTRIES THEIR FREEDOM. THERE IS MUCH HATE FOR THIS NATION. IN FACT, MORE HATE IN EASTERN EUROPE THAN IN YOUR COUNTRY."

"Why does man seem to destroy his environment?"

"HE WANTS TO DESTROY HIMSELF SUBCONSCIOUSLY DUE TO NEGATIVE THINKING. IF HE DESTROYS HIS PLANET HE WILL ONLY HAVE TO START AGAIN IN ANOTHER PLANET BECAUSE IT IS PART OF THE EVOLUTIONARY PROCESS AS LONG AS A PHYSICAL BODY VEHICLE IS NEEDED."

"IF MAN DEVELOPS TO HIS HIGHEST POTENTIAL THERE WILL BE NO NEED OF THE PHYSICAL BODY. THEY WILL BE AS OTHER BEINGS FROM OTHER WORLDS."

"What can we do for world peace?"

"PRAY EVERYDAY FOR IT! THAT IS THE BEST YOU CAN DO OUTWARDLY. BUT THE KEY IS TO BE PEACEFUL INWARDLY, OR IT MEANS LITTLE."

"Can spiritual growth lengthen life here on earth?"

"AS WE DEVELOP ALONG SPIRITUAL LINES, THINGS DO CHANGE, ACCORDING TO KARMA AND BURNING UP THE OLD. THEN YOU WILL BE FREE. WITH FREEDOM THERE IS MORE CHOICE. SOME CHOOSE TO LEAVE SOONER."

"SOME LEARN HOW TO STRENGTHEN THEIR LIFE FORCES TO PROLONG THEIR LIFE. WHOLESOME FOODS, WHOLESOME THOUGHTS, AND LEARNING MORE ABOUT DEEP BREATHING IS GOOD. RELEASE ANXIETIES."

"REMEMBER THAT SPIRITUAL GROWTH IS DETACHMENT, AND WILL LENGTHEN PHYSICAL LIFE IF YOU ARE A TRUE SERVANT. THEN YOU NEED NOT BE CONCERNED. IF YOU TAKE CARE OF YOU BODY AND MIND, ALL WILL EVOLVE NATURALLY AS PLANNED."

"THERE IS A GREAT BEING ALIVE TODAY LIKE JESUS, WHO IS SEVERAL HUNDRED YEARS OLD. HE LIVES IN THE HIMALAYAS AND IS SEEN BY A FEW ENLIGHTENED ONES. HE HAS REMAINED IN ORDER TO HELP KEEP SPIRITUAL BALANCE IN THE WORLD."

"Can anyone heal by sending out thoughts?"

"WE ALL HAVE THE POWER TO HEAL IF WE DEVELOP IT. IT IS NOT ABNORMAL. IF WE PUT OURSELVES ASIDE, AS AN INSTRUMENT FOR THE HIGHER. THERE ARE MANY THINGS WE WILL BE ABLE TO DO AS A RESULT. HEALING CAN TAKE PLACE BY JUST SENDING LIGHT AND LOVE TO THE PERSON OR ANIMAL. FOCUS THAT ENERGY. KEEP YOUR BODY HEALTHY IN SUCH A MANNER SO THAT IT CAN PERFORM."

"Why can't some be healed when they want to so bad?"

"THEY NEED TO BE MORE OF AN OPEN CHANNEL. MORE EFFECTIVE HEALING DEPENDS ON THE AMOUNT OF BARRIERS PUT UP TO BLOCK HOW MUCH HEALING FORCE GETS THROUGH. ONE CAN RAISE OR LOWER BARRIERS."

"Is it okay to love more than one Master, such as Jesus and Buddha?"

"THIS IS VERY WONDERFUL YET VERY HARD FOR MAN. BUT IF YOU CONTINUE TO BE OPEN AND LOVE ALL, YOU WILL GO BEYOND JUST MAN'S LIMITED CONCEPTS OF GOD. THE DEITIES KNOW THAT THE MOST IMPOR-

TANT THING IS NOT HAVING A FALSE GOD IN ONE, BUT LOVING ALL, AND TO LEARN ALL."

"Should time be spent alone to find out more about God?"

"IT MAY BE A DIFFICULT TASK TO BE ALONE, BUT IT IS A TRUE PRE-REQUISITE FOR REAL INITIATION INTO TRUE WISDOM. ALL GREAT SAGES AND BEINGS SPENT MUCH TIME IN SOLITUDE AND ALSO FACED THE SAME BATTLES WITH WORLD PLEASURES AND TEMPTATIONS, AS IN THIS TIME. IT IS MORE DIFFICULT IN THIS TIME ONLY BECAUSE THERE ARE SO ANY MATERIAL OPPORTUNITIES BECKONING. THE PAST HAD MORE STRUGGLE JUST FOR SURVIVAL AND SUSTENANCE. YOU HAVE SEEN BEFORE YOUR EYES THE POWER OF MATERIALISM. VERY FEW CAN REALLY CONTROL THIS POWER AND BE SPIRITUALLY GROUNDED: THEREFORE, BE CAREFUL WHEN YOU ASK FOR WEALTH, THAT THIS WEALTH BE THE TRUE WEALTH, SPIRITUAL WISDOM."

"REMEMBER, WE ARE ALL ALONE... AND NEVER ALONE. IT IS NOT POSSIBLE TO RELY ON ONE ANOTHER FOR HAPPINESS... FOR NO ONE BUT YOURSELF IS CAPABLE OF THAT TASK."

EPILOGUE

The preceding messages have all been recorded by tape, or written down as they came forth from Richard. As of this date, Richard, now thirty-three, has stepped back temporarily from the "world" and gone into semi-seclusion up north, by the redwoods, receiving more empowerments. He has made a total spiritual commitment to be a pure channel to help uplift man and his world.

We must realize how important it is for all of us to help in any way we can. By developing more inner peace and compassion we are helping not only ourselves, but our world, who so desperately needs it. We are just a small part, a grain of sand in the great universe. But every grain adds up to compose the whole.

It is time to look within, to where we really are going. If there is unhappiness in life then it is time to evaluate where we are.

When we 'cross over' we take our thoughts, our attitudes, and ourselves with us. If we want to be in more harmony and well being we must begin now to feel more inner peace. Open your own channel, let it in.

We all have the ability to 'tune in' to other souls, whether they are on earth, or in another realm. We need to clear away the debris of negativity that we have allowed in our consciousness -- in this lifetime, and from many lifetimes. It is so important to understand not only yourself, but the whole natural cycle of continual life.

Every effort each day, each minute we take to overcome some sense of negative thinking is a step to our spiritual growth.

We must remember, all souls yearn for love, peace and harmony, whether on this side, or beyond. As we send love out to our world and other worlds we are truly learning that we all are one, helping each other along the way. It is natural to communicate with each other here, or when we bridge over... to the 'other side'.

* * *

"I am certain that I have been here as I am now, a thousand times before, and I hope to return a thousand times... Man is the dialogue between nature and God. On other planets this dialogue will doubtless be of a higher and profounder character. What is lacking is self knowledge. After that the rest will follow."

J.W. von Goethe, Memoirs of Johannes Falk

"Once we accept the fact that authoritative information can come to us from sources beyond our earth – beyond the realm of ordinary laboratory proofs, we have gone far toward establishing a permanent pathway for our understanding."

James Crenshaw, "Telephone Between Worlds"

"It is the secret of the world that all things subsist and do not die, but only retire a little from sight, and afterward return again..."

Ralph Waldo Emerson

"I think immortality is the passing of a soul through man's lives or experiences, and such as are truly lived, used and learned, help on to the next, each growing richer, happier and higher, carrying with it only the real memories of what has gone before."

Louisa May Alcott

SUGGESTED READING

Bibliography

We Don't Die (Geo. Anderson's Conversations with the other side) J.Martin & P. Romanowski, G.P. Putnam, 1988
Opening to Channel, S.Roman & D.Parker, Kramer, 1987
Other Lives, Other Selves, Roger Woolger, PHD., Doubleday, 1987
Channeling, Jon Klimo, Jeremy Tarsher, St. Martins Press, 1987
Living Your Past Lives, K. Schlotterback, Ballantine, 1987
The Dead Are Alive, Harold Sherman, Fawcett Gold Medal, 1981, 1987
The God-Mind Connection, Jean Foster, Uni-Sun, 1987
Herald of the New Age, Ruth Montgomery, Doubleday/Dolphin, 1986
Lazarus, J. Purcell, Synergy Pub., 1986
A Matter of Personal Survival, "Life after Death", Michael Marsh Questbook/Theosophical Pub. House, 1985
Spirit Guides: We are Not Alone, Iris Belhayes, ASC Pub., 1985

Return From Death, Margot Grey, 1985
Life Between Life, Joel L. Whitton MD, PhD, J.Fisher, Warner, 1986
Dancing in the Light, Shirley Maclaine, Bantam, 1985
Afterlife, Colin Wilson, London: Harap, Ltd., 1985
Agartha: a Journey to the Stars, Meredith Lady Young, Stillpoint Pub. 1984
Dreamtime and Inner Space, Shambhala Pub., 1984
Meetings at the Lodge, Stephen Levine, Anchor Press, Doubleday
Reincarnation: A New Horizon in Science, Religion and Society, Sylvia Cranston & Carey Williams, Julian Press, 1984
The Case for Reincarnation, J. Fisher, Bantam Books, 1984

The Search for Yesterday: A critical Examination of the Evidence for Reincarnation, D. Scott Rogo, Prentice-Hall, 1985
Mediumship and Survival, A Century of Investigation, A. Gould London: Paladin/ Granada, 1983
The Truth About the Hereafter and Reincarnation, David Bassant Finbarr Books, England, 1982
Out of Body Experiences, Janet Lee Mitchell, PhD, Ballantine, 1981
The Super Beings, John R. Price, Quartus Books, 1981
The Psychic Beam to Beyond, Jane Boulton, DeVorss, 1983
Many Voices, Eileen Garrett, Harper & Row, 1974
No Goodbyes – A Trip into the Beyond, Adela Rogers St. John
Stairway to Heaven, Zecharia Sitchin, Avon Pub., 1980
To Hear the Angels Sing, Dorothy MacLean, Lorian press, 1980
Astral Projection, M. Denning & O. Phillips, Llewellyn Pub., 1980
Death to Rebirth, Manley P. Hall, Philosophical Research Soc., 1975
You Have Been Here Before, Edith Fiore, Ballantine, 1979
Reincarnation in Christianity, Geddes MacGregor, Quest, 1978
Christianity and Psychial Research, E. Garth Moore, Oxford Univ. Press, 1977
Experiencing Reincarnation, James S. Perkins, Shea Pub. House, 1977
Voices from Other Lives, Thorwald Dethlefsen, Evans & Co., 1976

Companions Along the Way, Ruth Montgomery, Popular Library, 1976

A Course in Miracles, Foundation for Inner Peace, Tiburon Co.

Here and There: Psychic Communicaton Between our World and the Next, P. Phillips and W. MacLeod, Corgi/Transworld, London, 1975

From Science to Seance, Geo. W. Meek, Regency, London, 1974

Twenty Cases Suggestive of Reincarnation, Ian Stevenson, 1974

Many Mansions, Gina Cerminara, Signet, 1978, 1950

Death and Reincarnation, Sri Chinmoy, 1974

Seth Speaks, Jane Roberts, Prentice-Hall, 1974

The History of Spiritualism, Vols. 1 and 2, Sir Conan Doyle, Arno Press, 1975

The Presence of Other Worlds, E. Swedenborg, W. Van Dusen, Harper and Row, 1974

The Other Side, Rev. Bishop J. Pike, Doubleday 1968

A World Beyond, Ruth Montgomery, Fawcette Crest Boos, 1972

We Live Many Lives, Robert E. Smith, Paperback Library, 1971

Voices of Spirit Through the Psychic Experiences of Elwood Babitt, Chas. Hopgood, Leisure/Norton, 1975

The Spiritual Hierechies, Rudolph Steiner, Garber/Steiner Books 1970

Learning to Talk to the World Beyond, Ralph Knight, Stackpole, 1969

Altered States of Consciousness, Chas. Tart, J. Wiley & Sons, 1963

A Search for the Truth, Ruth Montgomery, Bantam Books, 1968

Here and Hereafter, Ruth Montgomery, DeVorss, 1970

Past Lives, Future Loves, Dick Sutphen, Rocket Books, 1978

On Death and Dying, E. Kubler-Ross, M.D, MacMillan Pub. 1970

During Sleep (co-operation between the living & dead) Robt. Crookall BSC, DSC Phd, University Books, 1974

Edgar Cayce on Reincarnation, Noel Langley, ARE Foundation, 1967

Parallel Paths to the Unseen Worlds, Felix Frazer, Builders of Adytum, Ptd., 1967

Window to the Past, Hans Holzer, Doubleday, 1969

Life in the World Unseen, Anthony Borgia, Corgi, Transworld Pub. London, 1966

The Belief in Life After Death, C.J.Ducasse, C. Thomas, 1961

Automatic Writing, an Approach to the Unconscious, A.Muhl, Garrett Pub., 1963

Venture Inward, Hugh Lynn Cace, Harper & Row, 1964

Between Two Worlds, Nandor Fodor, Parker Pub., 1964

Enigma oI Survival, Prof. Hornall Hart, 1969

Cosmic Memory, Rudolph Steiner, Garber/Steiner Books, 1959

The Search for Bridey Murphy, M. Bernstein, Doubleday, 1956

Nothing so Strange, A. Ford/M.H. Bro, Harper & Row, 1958

A Dweller on Two Planets; Phylos the Thebetan, Bordon Pub. 1952

The Case for Psychic Survival, Hereward Carrington, Citadel Press, 1957

Religion, Philosophy, Psychical Reasearch, C.D. Broad, Harcourt, Brace and World, 1953

Human Personality and it's Survival after Bodily Death, F.W. Myers, University Books, 1961

Telepathy of the Etheric Vehicle, Alice A. Bailey, Luis Pub., 1950

Telephone Between Worlds, James Crenshaw, DeVorss, 1950

IF YOU WISH TO CONTACT RICHARD
FOR SPIRITUAL OR ASTROLOGY READINGS
OR SPIRIT COMMUNICATIONS

WRITE TO: "RICHARD"
P.O. BOX 296
TRINIDAD, CA 95570

OR FOR FURTHER INFORMATION
WRITE VIKEE VAUGHN % THE ABOVE ADDRESS

CASSETTE TAPES AVAILABLE TO ORDER:
Send $8.95 Plus Postage to Above Address

MEDITATION/MUSIC TAPES

Dissolving Grief
Releasing - Negativity
　　　　　　The Past
Healing The Mind And Body
Magical Journey (for children)